Keys for Your JOURNEY

Unlocking Victory in Everyday Battles

DR. YVETTE AVERY

Dedication

To Ashley,
who inspires me
to honor my dreams
and
inspire others
through my journey.

Pecan Tree Publishing
www.pecantreebooks.com

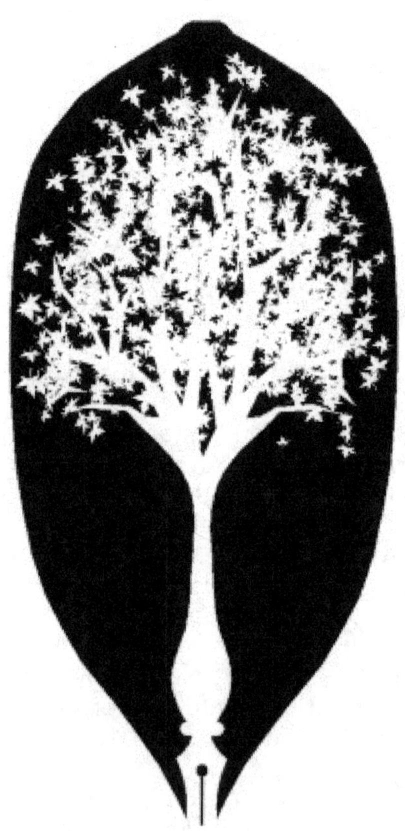

New Voices | New Styles | New Vision –
Creating a New Legacy of Dynamic
Authors and Titles
Hollywood, FL

Contents

Introduction

One night I found myself in a dream that was so clear it seemed as though I was actually there walking through the experience. I was not scared; but I was struck by the profound blaring sound of alarms sounding off throughout the dream. When the dream opens, I am in front of a grated door and a tall, powerful, shrouded figure (like the archangel Michael) accompanies me. In the dream I am the owner of keys to every door in the building; and the only one who has these keys. Initially, I do not know how or why I have the keys. My archangel companion keeps reminding me that my keys unlock everything I need. As I move forward in the dream, I use the keys. I run into varying situations in which people in the dream need access to something. When I encounter the different situations, my companion encourages me to select a key to unlock what that person or persons are encountering. Every person I encounter keeps saying to me, "But I do not have the key." Again, the voice reminds me, "You have all the keys that you need." So, one by one as I run into these various people who need access, I select a key to open their situation. One person needed the key to unlock a box that holds information. Another person needed to gain movement up a hill. This dream goes through various scenarios. It becomes clear to me without the key for access, having an opportunity or situation is meaningless. Each person had everything they needed but the key that opened that door. Not having the key prevented them from moving forward through the door.

These keys that I share will help you unlock the situations you encounter. My journey takes place as a teacher, my calling in Christ. Your journey may be as a teacher as well, or as an entrepreneur, doctor, speaker, it does not really matter because these keys can unlock the journey you are on. In Christ, you have everything that you already need even the keys to The Kingdom.

KEY ONE

Prayer is Always in Season

Prayer is the key that unlocks every situation that we will encounter. It is also probably the most neglected area of our spiritual lives. Everything, including all of life's situations, starts with prayer. Open your day with prayer. The Lord's Prayer (Matthew 6:10-14) is the most complete prayer. Jesus taught His disciples this prayer and all others in The Bible are supplemental to this one. It covers everything you will need to start your day and direct you throughout the day. If you study this prayer, you will notice it starts with God, then moves to God's purpose for this Earth, our provision, forgiveness, temptation, protection from evil, God's power and authority, and glory for eternity. I pray this daily, and I pray it into matters as God directs. Prayer can never have an end or a beginning. Paul said pray without ceasing; and guess what, in this life you do need to pray all the time.

So, as we start our day, let us pray:

> *"Our Father in heaven, Hallowed be Your name.*
> *Your kingdom come. Your will be done. On Earth as it is in heaven.*
> *Give us today our daily bread.*
> *And forgive us our debts. As we forgive our debtors.*

> *And do not lead us into temptation.*
> *But deliver us from the evil one.*
> *For Yours is the Kingdom and the power*
> *and the glory forever. Amen." (Matthew*
> *6:10-14, New American Standard Bible/*
> *NASB)*

Each new day, I commit myself to the will of The Father on this Earth, to be on duty, watch for the children that I teach, and manage the roles and responsibilities given me. I commit myself to prayer because nothing else will matter if I do not. My assignment on this Earth is a call of God; without God I can do nothing. There is never a day I will start without committing myself to prayer, giving my day to God, and allowing God to lead me in what I pray.

My prayer time in the morning spans from the time I am up and sometimes will carry over into the car. I do not have music playing or a favorite prayer warrior on the line; it is just me and The Father. Words from God will overflow these prayers and I can hear The Father's heart in whatever is going on around me. Some days I am given a specific burden. Thus, I might pray for revelation. That the things that are hidden in the dark be brought to the light. I might pray Godly sight into the unknown to see before a plan is even in operation. I might ask God to give me His heart for the children entrusted to me. Some days I am given a name of a child or a family, but all prayers are welcomed. Then some days a scripture is laid on my heart. For years as a teacher, I prayed the same *scripture Psalm 19:14 (New King James Version/ NKJV)*, "Let the words of my mouth and the meditation of my heart be acceptable in your sight. My Lord and My redeemer." The prayers are never the same because every day is a new day. Everyday there is something new going on and I have to be aware of it all to be prepared for my day. I am preparing for an unseen battle.

Years ago, I was in a teacher exchange program for my school in a Muslim nation, Azerbaijan. My school was a partnering institution and I volunteered to represent my educational institution with five students for the year. As part of my mission, I am always drawn to reaching people who others have either overlooked or forgotten. Prior to this time, I participated in missions' trips, so for me this was an answer to my prayers. Despite all the obstacles I could encounter I knew God had called me to go. My school staff was actually very apprehensive, and no one really wanted to continue this partnership. I was bubbling with excitement when the opportunity was announced. Without hesitation I volunteered but I would have to confirm hosting the teacher with my family and make a trip to Russia for a month. The obstacles, or should I say the spiritual battles, were constant once I stepped foot in the country, but God always prevailed. To even sleep I had to spend half my night praying ceaselessly to fight off men in dark shadows (demons) that would come at night to wrestle with me, sit on me, or try to smother me. The only rest I could get was when the one tape I had of prophetic worship music was playing. When that tape would end those demons would start up again and I would turn the tape over and start it again. No one even knew the kind of nights I was having and as the time continued, I was bolder with those demons, and they became less. God gave me the words to defeat them, and they were very afraid of the name of Jesus when I spoke out against them. They would scream, cover their ears, and shrink away.

In that country I learned a newfound power of prayer like I have never experienced in my life. There was no church or prayer partner, no radio or even a Bible bookstore, just me and Jesus. In Azerbaijan, the call to prayer happened every day at noon. When I first heard the minaret, the Muslim's call to prayer, sounding off, I thought there might be an emergency, then I noticed people from around the neighborhood walking toward the sound. My host informed me that every day the religious Muslims pray at least three times daily using a call to prayer. They stopped everything. People came from all walks of life to pray three times a day. I thought I am not praying enough. No wonder the forces of darkness think they can get ahead of me; I am not taking them as seriously as I should. It was then I decided to change my prayer throughout the day. We hear about the prophet Daniel in *Psalm 55:16-17 (NKJV)* praying three times a day, *"As for me, I shall call upon God, And the Lord will save me. Evening and morning and at noon, I will complain and murmur, And He will hear my voice."* Prayer invites God into everything that happens on this Earth, *"Your kingdom come as it is in heaven,"* (Matthew 6:10, NASB).

As a result of this experience, I commit my lunch time at school to prayer. My noon day prayer is different from the morning. It is a prayer of intercession for my students individually. As I intercede on behalf of my students the Lord brings me their concerns, struggles, and pains. Sometimes I meditate on a scripture. During the midday prayer, I listen and wait for The Father to hear his words of knowledge about my students. As I pray, I walk around my class worshipping with music, singing praises which transitions me into a deeper intercession of prayer. It is at that time I get the opportunity to hear a word for my students to direct my prayers as I move to compassion for them. Sometimes, I find myself weeping for them without really knowing why I am crying. I would hear there is family unemployment, someone is sick, or they are having hard times at home, or no one is there for them. Years ago, the Lord reminded me that not everyone has someone praying for them. I grew up in a family of praying women and if I was not praying, I knew my mother or grandmother were. So, I pray for my students because I could be the only one seeking God for them.

My prayers for my future students begin in the summer before school even starts. As the summer progresses, I send up prayers to The Father. God's Word says, *"A man's heart plans his way, but the Lord directs his steps,"* (Proverbs 16:9, NKJV). In *Proverbs 19:21 (NKJV)* it continues with, *"There are many plans in a man's heart, Nevertheless the Lord's counsel—that will stand."* All my planning, even my summer strategy, the Lord directs. I invite the Lord to counsel me in my plans, direct my steps, and the plans that others are making for my classes.

Prayer

Thank you for this day, Lord. I commit my day to You. I lift my plans You have for me. Give me the wisdom that I need to do all that you have for me to do. Open my eyes so I can have the revelation I need in every situation I will face today. You are my Father, and You always want the best for me in every situation that I must face. Bless my going out and my coming in. Give me the insight and wisdom to do all that you have given me to do this day.
In Jesus' name, Amen

How do I know the way of the Lord? I connect my spirit to The Father in prayer throughout every moment of my day.

A Fresh Word

Prayer is communicating with God. God is always near to hear our prayers, requests, and even complaints. God has always communicated with mankind. From the very beginning we see God and man communicating, *"Then the Lord God called to the man, and said to him, 'Where are you?' He said, 'I heard the sound of You in the garden, and I was afraid because I was naked; so, I hid myself',"* (Genesis 3:9-10, NASB). Man's communication with God continues, even after Adam, with the next generation of Seth and his son Enosh in *Genesis 4:24* (NASB) calling out to the Lord, *"Then men began to call on the name of the Lord,"*.

God communicates with man with a fresh word every day. If you were to survey the different religions you will find that prayer is always a staple, what varies is who the person will pray to, and that is what makes all the difference. There is only one God, the true and living God; and throughout history He is known for keeping His promises. In *Psalms 65:2* (NKJV) we find, "And to You the [a]vow shall be performed. O You who hear prayer." Prayer is a vowed deed and God hears our prayers. God's house is a house of prayer for all nations.

A day without prayer eliminates the opportunity for the spirit to help me in my weaknesses. The Spirit searches our hearts and knows how to intercede for us according to the will of The Father. One may not know how to pray, but the spirit pleads our case to The Father's will for us *(Romans 8:27, NKJV).* Daily God searches our hearts to give us what is the mind of the Spirt. As in any relationship communication, prayer, can change the direction of the situation. My prayers acknowledge my need of The Father and my submission to His sovereignty over my life.

Have you had a relationship with a person in which you noticed communication was difficult, stymied, or worst –

nonexistent? You do not know what they want; they do not know what is bothering you. Then finally someone hits a boiling point, a crisis, and guess what disaster ensues. In relationships someone is the communicator, and the other person is the recipient. In our relationship with God, He is both receiver and communicator. In your communication with God do not allow yourself to be a talking head with a long list of requests and petitions. Remember true communication includes both parties, and God has a fresh word to communicate to you daily. Be a listener as well.

In my daily prayers God will give me direction or simply drop a prayer in my heart for someone or a situation. Sometimes God will give me directions, prayers, or unpredictable prayers. One morning God woke me up and I was already praying. I had a night full of dream activity.

In the dream there was an exceptionally large school with several buildings. In the courtyard, there was a loud alarm bell going off. This loud bell disturbed me. In the school office people were rushing out. I was going through the building with keys, opening, and locking doors; someone was traveling with me, a large male person. I never saw his face, but he kept encouraging me to use the keys to go to the various parts of this school. It was not the school that I worked for, but I would go to one door, open it, and lock the door behind me, so no one else could get into the area. All the while that loud bell was sounding off. I never really encountered children, but by the time the dream ended I was on the first floor. I had started on the third floor and at the end of it I found myself in the cleared-out office area except for a male administrator that was running back and forth.

When I woke up from the dream, I was praying. My prayers were urgent, and the words seemed to overflow from my spirit. I was crying and pleading, praying for students who were not necessarily mine. After a while I blurted out, "Something is going to happen at a school today." I kept praying but began crying for the safety and well-being of the students and teachers involved. Later that day I found out about the Valentine's Day shooting in Parkland, Florida. In six minutes, a former student killed seventeen people, students and two teachers.

We may not know how to pray or know the mind of the spirit, but we are to pray and seek the will of The Father even in our prayers. Prayer is not a request, or an option, but a requirement. Jesus said

> *"When you pray the smoke of the incense are the prayers of the saints ascend before God from the angels' hand," Revelation 8:4 (NKJV). Our prayers are golden bowls of incense that flood the altar of God with our requests and petitions. They reach heaven and the throne of God daily.*

> *Genesis 4:26 (NKJV)– "Then men began to call on the name of the Lord."*

> *Romans 8:26 (NKJV)– "We do not know what we should pray, but the spirit himself pleads our case with unexpressed groans."*

> *Matthew 6:6 (NKJV) – "But when you pray, go to your room, shut the door, and pray to your Father who is present in that secret place. Your Father who sees what you do in secret will reward you."*

| Prayer |

Lord, help me in my weaknesses and guide me in my prayers. Teach me how to pray Your will and the heart of The Father. I commit my prayers to the will of The Father on this Earth. Thank you for Your Spirit that teaches me everything that I need. No weapon formed against me shall prosper and every tongue that rises against me in judgment I condemn. I take the shield of faith and quench every fiery dart of the enemy.
Amen

How do I pray the will of The Father? I pray His Word.

Pray The Word

Prayer has always been the center of my life. From my early years praying in the upper room, (the church attic above the sanctuary), to serving in the prayer ministry, prayer has always been my center piece. I have always loved communing with God. From my experience as a prayer counselor and intercessor most people do not pray because they believe there is a special formula to prayer or feel inadequate to pray. Some will even say, "I don't even know where to begin in prayer." This honest response has led many to leave prayer to someone else or not pray at all. This self-made criterion has left many confused, frustrated, and hopeless. We flutter in our confusion stabbing in the darkness trying to figure out how to pray. *James 4:3 (NKJV)* notes, *"You do not have because you do not ask. You ask and do not receive, because you ask amiss."* To end the confusion on how to pray – we must simply pray The Word of God.

Pray The Word of God which simply means pray the written scripture. Praying the scripture is a quick short cut to prayer. I feel you asking, "But what if I do not know The Word? Do I not pray? Will my prayers go unanswered?" No one has been born with The Word of God in their heart or memory. We all start somewhere. I can remember being doubtful about my capacity to memorize The Word. The Word is amazing because even if you only know a few scriptures the spirit will remind you of The Word. The Word is truth.

Years ago, when I was a freshman in college, I decided I would reinvent myself, after all who knew me. I would go to school, do what I wanted, and no one would know that I had a relationship with God. My first sign that God was not going to leave me alone started with the Christian club on campus. I was definitely not joining, but they kept asking me to join them. I always stood my ground and said no. Then the group started meeting in my dorm suite and again would try to get me in their conversation. Finally, they convinced me to serve on the board but not be an active member. My position required me to provide outreach for the club. So, I would spend days setting up services and transportation inviting religious guests to the campus and serving as the guests' host. I never attended any of these meetings I was not a member, but meanwhile I was in constant contact and conversation with youth pastors, churches, and religious teachers seeking to serve the college community for outreach. Then one Sunday I was invited to attend the only religious service on campus the Catholic Mass. I was never a Catholic in my Christian experience but for some reason my roommate asked me to go with her. She made the excuse that she didn't want to go alone. Well, the attendance seemed innocuous to me so I went a couple of more times thinking I could hide there. The third Sunday I attended; the priest called me to his study after service. He told me that I didn't belong there. He said I knew what I needed to do to know God and attending Mass was not the way. I wondered what he knew about me, so I never went back. More things kept drawing me to God. I would find myself hanging out with people at a party and someone would inevitably turn and say, "You don't belong here." At first, I was confused but it kept happening usually followed by, "This is not you." I was doing what they were doing but they pointed out that I should not be there. Well as the semester moved forward God made it increasingly difficult for me to hide. One night about midway into my first college semester He called me from my hiding to publicly announce that I was indeed a believer and His child in Christ. At the time my friend, a new believer, was in a spiritual battle with the enemy who refused to let her go. I woke up to screams and crying from her room. God told me to go in her room and pray. When I asked her to open the door she did despite the efforts of other friends and school security before me. I prayed Psalms 23, the only prayer I recalled after 18 years in the church, over her life. I prayed that scripture the whole night as God instructed me. I knew many scriptures, but God knew the scripture, the prayer she needed at that time. This is where I learned The Word is a sword against the enemy.

The Word is called truth. Truth is not debatable; it is a fact. It does not fail; it is infallible. If I do not know the truth, how can I know what to ask, how can I know what is truly available for me. The Word is like unclaimed money. There is a government department in every state that holds unclaimed money from its past and deceased residents. Who would leave their money to the state government and not claim it? Different circumstances may have that money go unclaimed, but I think the most prevalent one is the person who dies, and the family does not know about the money, or the person has lost contact with their family. How long will the government hold this money? I am not sure, but personally I have seen 25 years or more. The power is there, the truth is there, but untapped, unclaimed the prayer remains unasked for leaving the praying person defeated and discouraged. *Matthew 22:29 (New International Version /NIV)* Jesus replied to the religious leaders, *"You are in error because you do not know the scriptures or the power of God. Just praying is not effective if we pray amiss."*

"This is the confidence we have in approaching God: that if we ask anything according to His will, He hears us. And if we know that He hears us—whatever we ask—we know that we have what we asked of Him," First John *5:14-15 (NIV).* The Word promises that our prayers have answers, and we can confidently approach God if we pray according to His will. What is the will of The Father? The answer is in His Word.

Read The Word and find out the prayers of The Father. The more you read, I promise, the more you will want to know.

Reading The Word is like a personal journey with The Father. When I first became a student of The Word, I was afraid of the Old Testament, so I read the New Testament. I wanted to walk in Jesus' shoes and see how He lived. But as time continued, I sought different pathways of study according to the drawing of the spirit in my life. The Word never grows old, even if you read the same word all day by the evening, I can promise you it will be different. The Word is like peeling an onion layer after layer as you dig further into it. In *Second Timothy 3:16 (NIV)* says, *"All Scripture is God-breathed and is useful for teaching, rebuking, correcting and training in righteousness."* Armed with The Word you will not miss any of the promises and truths God has for you.

> *John 7:38 (NASB) – "Whoever believes in me, as Scripture has said, rivers of living water will flow from within them."*

Mark 12:24 (NASB) – "Jesus replied, "Are you not in error because you do not know the Scriptures or the power of God?"

Second Timothy 3:16 (NASB) - "All Scripture God-breathed and is useful for teaching, rebuking, correcting, and training in righteousness."

Prayer

There is power in every word spoken in Your name. Teach me the prayers of Your heart so I can know more about You and Your will. May Your Word teach me truth; reveal to me the mysteries of Your Word on every level of my life. Thank you for the power of Your Word to transform every situation in my life.
Amen

How do I pray to The Father? I ask according to The Word.

To pray The Word, you can state the scripture and use your name or the person you are praying for in the verse. For example, *"Our Father I pray that You will supply all that I need according to Your riches in glory by Christ Jesus,"* (Philippians 4:19, NKJV).

Another example may sound like this, *"Father, may I forget those things which are behind and reach forward to those things which are ahead. May I press toward the goal for the prize of the upward call of God in Christ Jesus,"* (Philippians 3:13-14, NKJV).

Prayer, Praise, and Revelation

Pursue prayer. We access our authority to come against destruction, sickness, defeat, and any works of the enemy, darkness through prayer and confession, praise, and thanksgiving. We must contend with the works of darkness and operate in our given power and authority. David has a long tumultuous history. He is anointed by Samuel (as a young boy) to be king, appointed as King Saul's armourbearer, kills Goliath, defeating the Philistines, and committing adultery with Bathsheba to murder. He is also the writer and psalmist of the Book of Psalms that records the high and lows of his relationship to others, his enemies, and God. David understood the power of prayer starting in *Psalm 2: 8 (NKJV). "Ask of Me and I will give you the nations for Your inheritance, And the ends of the Earth for Your possession."* In *Psalm 3:4 (NKJV)*, David asks for divine protection, *"I cried to the Lord with my voice, And He heard me from His holy hill."* We see the prayers of David in victory after victory over his enemies. His Psalms show that we must be persistent, consistent in seeking the Lord, making our supplication known to Him, and praying The Word. Our enemies are not the person but the spiritual forces of darkness that can come against us. One of my sure-fire ways to pursue prayer is my personal prayer list. I call it my 'hit list' because every day I am hitting that list praying for the people on it. The list ranges from people I know to even those I do not know. I have had supervisors, family members, children, parents to even stories I have seen in the news to pray about on the list. I keep track of them somehow and record the outcomes as it unfolds.

There are times when we wonder what can I do? What should I be doing? If you have not prayed, then there is not much to do until you do. I pray about everything and sometimes I say to God this might be a silly request, but I need your guidance, your wisdom, and I pray. You know what I have discovered? God hears every prayer that we make, and He never judges them. Pursue prayer means go after it, seek it, keep at it until you cannot and continue again. *Romans 12:2, (NKJV)* tells us *"...rejoicing in hope, patient[a] in tribulation, continuing steadfastly in prayer..."* Sometimes people will say, "I prayed but I didn't see anything change or happen." So ends the prayer life at that point. They have stopped believing in the transforming power of God. God is God and what we see with our physical sight limits our spiritual sight. We cannot see gravity, but we certainly know it is working, so do not get stuck questioning how God is working. David in *Psalm 4: 5, (NKJV)* says, *"...put your trust in the Lord."* Pursuing means nothing stops until you reach the accomplished goal. Pursue prayer and make confession.

Confession is praise, thanks to God. Praising is part of our prayers. David says in *Psalms 4:7-8, (NKJV)* *"You have put gladness in my heart...For you alone, O Lord, make me dwell in safety."* Then in *Psalm 5: 11 (NIV)* David proclaims, *"Let those also who love Your name be joyful in You."* Prayer is not just a matter of asking, but praising God, and thanking Him. We miss out when we see prayer only as a list of wants to The Father. Throughout The Word we see that prayer, supplication and praise go hand in hand. Do you know what happens in your heart when you praise the Lord? It encourages you. It reminds you of His endless possibilities, His history. For years, as I have shared, I have kept a prayer journal. The journal started with me praying my hit list but in time I realized the importance of reminding myself of the answers God has provided over the course of my life. I call those answers 'stones of remembrance'. Remember when the Jews crossed over the Jordan? Joshua told the people, *"Each of you is to take up a stone on his shoulder, according to the number of the tribes of the Israelites, to serve as a sign among you… These stones are to be a memorial to the people of Israel forever,"* *(Joshua 4:5-6, NASB).* When I praise the Lord, it makes me realize the smallness of my situation compared to what God has done. Glorify God and seek Him in praise. How do I praise the Lord? What are the words that I can use in my praise? My praises come from thanking God for who He is, His promises, and what He has already done in my life.

Every year there is this rush to commit to reading The Bible by some believers and then in other situations the only one opening The Bible is the pastor. The Word is manna to your soul, spiritual food; without The Word you lack the power and strength necessary in this life to combat the evil one and his tactics. The Bible is God's revelation of Himself and His will for man. There are different literary forms embodied in The Bible: poetry, songs, letters, speeches, to name a few, but only one source - God. The Bible is timeless and trustworthy. The apostles used the Old Testament, which we still use today, to teach about Jesus Christ. Christ prophesized The Word and the fulfilling of scripture still happens today. The apostles' writing follows the same format. Prophecies in The Bible are direct and come to pass.

Lastly, The Word is powerful and transformative. I share The Word every day in my classroom. No, I do not read The Bible to my class or shout from the podium "Thus sayeth the Lord," but I realized a long time ago that The Word is a seed I get to plant in every student's life I encounter. So, by knowing The Word I can use it daily in my classroom and plant that seed to transform lives. I will easily share a scripture imparting wisdom with my students because The Word tells me it will not come back void. I get a real kick out of doing this and as a result I have memorized more

Word because of it. Students at times will recognize the power of the wisdom and remark how deep or profound my words are to them. I love it because they are going to remember that Word and a seed has been planted that could change their life.

Our prayers come from The Word. I am not suggesting to just idly memorize The Bible but realize how to pray starts with reading The Word. In *Matthew 22:29 (NKJV)*, Jesus answered and said to them, *"You are [a]mistaken, not knowing the scriptures nor the power of God."* The Word will transform how you pray because you will know God and His power. Praying The Word proclaims His faithfulness and truth to everything that concerns us. Pray The Word and see the revelation of God in your life.

> *Psalm 2: 8 (NKJV)- "Ask of Me and I will give you the nations for Your inheritance, And the ends of the Earth for Your possession."*

> *Matthew 22:29 (NKJV) – "You are [a] mistaken, not knowing the Scriptures nor the power of God."*

> *Second Timothy 3:16 (NKJV) – "All Scripture is given by the inspiration of God."*

> *Ephesians 6:18 (NKJV)– "Praying always with all prayer and supplication in the spirit, being watchful to this end with all perseverance and supplication for all the saints."*

Prayer

Lord, teach me how to pray today. From my heart I praise You and all that You have done for me. Your undying love and care for me overwhelms me. Thank you for always interceding on behalf of me. I am pursuing Your Word in my life. The Earth proclaims everything in Your will today. You are the joy of my salvation. Refresh Your Spirit in me, so I may serve You in every part of my life. Grant me the heart to hear and the eyes to see the needs that surround me, so I can be an extension of You on this Earth. May I not grow slack in anything You have given me to do; I am more alive than I have ever been.
Amen

How are my prayers heard? I pray The Word and He fulfills His Word.

KEY TWO

Power in the spirit

Endowed by The Spirit to do
Even Greater Things

We all want to leave a mark; something to be remembered for good while we are alive or dead. The Word says that what we do will outlive our lives on this Earth. I remember saying as a young woman in college, "I want to do something big. I want people to remember me long after I am gone." When I pictured this, I remembered I envisioned a famous novel, a world classic, something material, after all I was going to be a famous writer. I imagined something great, some grand accomplishment, but my vision was small even when I thought it was big. God gives us more than we can conceptualize. God has given me greater than I imagined. When I thought about big, I never visualized I would teach students for over three decades in two different states, in three different countries, and students from over twenty different countries. I never can take credit for any of my teaching except my willingness to embrace all of it. In the years that I have taught English in public schools I have taught a small country of people which continues to grow and gives back from the watering that God allowed me to provide.

The Spirit has been my guide through it all. How can I leave a mark when I can barely keep track of me? I am teacher, mentor, and often parent for the students. Yes, there have been times when the job to reach back and pull so many ahead seemed beyond impossible. In my weakness God has become strong and stronger in my life. I must hold onto Him because He is the source of all our strength. God is my strength, and He alone can make my call possible. I can remember times of absolute helplessness and defeat. I prayed for the Lord to move this out of my life. I prayed against that stronghold or belief. Holy Spirit come; Holy Spirit lead me today in everything that I do.

The enemy will always want to distract you with the physical; that which is right in front of you. As a teacher that distraction can be many things: a child, a state test, a disgruntled parent, or yourself. Do not let the enemy distract you; your battle is not the flesh and blood, but spirit and only The Holy Spirit can direct you through that battle. Hold out for The Spirit to overcome and see how He will triumph.

One of my jobs in education was a curriculum support specialist position in the district office for the advanced students in secondary schools. I loved that job because I was in a constant learning state and truthfully dependent on the spirit for everything. Even when I applied for the position, I was trying to get another job at another school. In the process of finalizing the position at the school with a final interview the district office contacted me to interview for the position. It was crazy because even when I got the call I was confused because I was still thinking it was the school.

I could have never been prepared for the next challenge in my position. Suddenly outside of the classroom I was required to support teachers and administrators across the county and at the same time enforce district policies and requirements for advanced students. Day by day The Spirit would guide me in my job tasks even though I had no knowledge just an incredible willingness and openness to serve the teachers and students. It was a mission for me to reach the underserved students and schools. I have always worked in top rated schools in the district, but I felt the call to reach out for the many who still never knew those experiences in the vast district. I left the cushioned school because I wanted to maximize not just my students' opportunities but as many students, teachers, and schools as possible.

My first assignment on the job took me to present the budget plan from the district to an audience of administrators and address any questions or concerns. I had never spoken to a roomful of administrators from across the county even though I am teacher. All I could do was pray and trust The Spirit. I was given the assignment the day after I joined the office. I not only presented the plan; the administrators were gracious and the questions I could not address I noted for follow up. The meeting was one of so many and every time The Spirit triumphed and took me along in the process. I could not rely on myself because every requirement for the job that I considered an obstacle, a weakness for me, was required for me on that job.

The Holy Spirit was always the one single voice guiding and directing me. Without The Spirit I would have never ventured so boldly into so many unknown territories. I know with The Spirit I can do even greater things than I can even imagine and that is why I start each morning with The Holy Spirit. The Holy Spirit is the greatest teacher, confidante, and friend that I could ever have now and always.

> *Exodus 35:31 (NKJV)- "Spirit of God in wisdom, understanding, and knowledge and all craftsmanship."*

John 14:26 (NKJV)- "He will teach you all things."

John 16:13 (NKJV)- "The Spirit of truth, guide you into all truth."

> **Prayer**
>
> *Thank you, Lord, for Your power that you have given me. Your power that only The Holy Spirit can give is beyond the scope of my enemies. Fill me afresh with Your Spirit this day. I want to be led by You to do the works that You have designed for me. Your Spirit leads me and guides me every step of my way. My life is in Your hands. Teach me the way that I should go.*
> *Amen*

How can I be greater? It is by the power of The Holy Spirit.

Power is always equated with strength, control, but in The Kingdom of God power is submission, obedience submitting to God's power. I increase in power not by controlling my world, but by eliminating my hold on all of it to The Spirit. How can I do this? Paul, the learned scholar, and disciple says in *Second Corinthians 12:10 (NKJV), "For when I am weak, He is strong."* Paul could easily brag about his knowledge and his abilities, but he calls our attention that his weaknesses, kept him from being proud, it humbled him. His weakness allowed for The Holy Spirit to work through him. The adventure of discovering starts with releasing your hold on all that you can do to The Spirit who can do more than what you think is possible. When you only see your life through your lens you have tunnel vision or worse, no vision at all. Stop trying to hold in the reins to what God can do in you.

Gifts with Returns

When I think about a gift, two things come to my mind. One, all the gifts that I have ever gotten were never the ones I asked for. My upbringing taught me not to complain, quietly accept the gift, less I be ungrateful. As a result, I have had countless gifts I never wanted. And yes, I have always received those gifts and never made a stink about them. I have used them wholeheartedly and unfortunately; they have a long-life expectancy. Then, there are gifts that I have received that were perfect, better than I really expected. Those loved gifts are reminders of how much love went into the decision. Sadly, those gifts have not been as plentiful as I would want.

The Holy Spirit also gives gifts. *"There are different kinds of gifts, but the same Spirit distributes them. There are different kinds of service, but the same Lord. There are different kinds of working, but in all of them and in everyone it is the same God at work,"* (First Corinthians 12: 4-7, NIV). The Spirit gives according to His will *(Hebrews 2:4, NIV)*. So, is there a difference between what the spirit gives me and my gift givers? Yes, absolutely! When the spirit gives this gift, I am foremost in His mind. I was created with that gift in mind. Now you may get a gift also that you may not initially embrace, but The Word says He will give you the desires of your heart. So, hang in there you will come to embrace that gift even in time. Secondly, His gifts are irrevocable; no one can take that gift away even if you are a poor steward of the gift. Yes, you may desire another gift like I have, but guess what God encourages us that all the gifts are of equal importance. We should desire the greatest gift - love *(First Corinthians 12: 31, NIV)* and He will show you a more excellent way.

Do I walk away from the gift that the spirit gives and feel ignored or appreciated? Even though the spirit gives us our gifts we cannot claim the gift from our best efforts. It is a gift that makes me unique from anyone else. No two gifts are the same because our gifts are personal. Even if someone has the same gift it will not be the same. Gifts are for ministering to the body, the church. So, I do not personally own this gift, but I am responsible to pray, seek, and grow in the gifts given by the spirit.

> *Hebrews 2:4 (NIV) "God also testified to it by signs, wonders and various miracles, and by gifts of The Holy Spirit distributed according to his will."*

> *First Corinthians 14:12 (NIV) "So it is with you. Since you are eager for gifts of the Spirit, try to excel in those that build up the church."*

> *First Corinthians 14:1 (NIV) "Follow the way of love and eagerly desire gifts of the Spirit, especially prophecy."*

> *First John 2:27 (NKJV) "But the anointing which you have received from Him abides in you, and you do not need that anyone teach you; but as the same anointing teaches you concerning all things, and is true, and is not a lie, and just as it has taught you, you [a]will abide in Him."*

Prayer

Thank You for all the gifts You have given me. They are for me. Lord, I want to be responsible for every gift that You have given me. Teach me how to deeply understand every dimension so I may grow, deeply rooted in the gift. Show me how I can be brilliant in the gift that You have given to bring glory to You and to build the body of Christ. Teach me the anointing that I have received from You. You are my teacher. You teach me all things that I need to know is true and is not a lie.
Amen

How do I grow in my gifts? I receive the gift and seek The Holy Spirit.

The question that you might have at this time might be how do I know the gift I have? How can I know my gift from other things I can do or like to do? There are spiritual gift surveys that you can take to assess your spiritual gifts, or you can reflect on your life and examine what is or has been operating in your life. Answering some reflective questions may get you to identify your gifts. What is your passion? What moves you or excites you? What do you naturally do or seek in your own personal time or interests? What are some patterns, pivotal moments you have observed over your lifetime about yourself?

For me there have been pivotal points in my life that helped me to identify my gifts. As a child I was always writing journals and journals full of poetry and reflections. I have never stopped writing. I have always been an avid nonfiction reader because I wanted to learn. Another significant gift throughout my life has been my prophetic dream life. My prophetic dreams have served as intercessory points of prayer which ties into my gift of intercession and prayer. My gift of teaching emerges over time in my life. No, I didn't play school, but I was always considered a know-it-all by my parents. At the time it was of course a point of correction but in reflection my know-it- all was my ability to be insightful and informative to everyone. I have always been able to talk to people and win their confidence even adults. Teaching came as a natural ability for me. During my teaching internship the school placed me in every classroom and detention hall they could. At the end of the internship, I was offered a job by the principal. If I look over my life all my gifts emerged and developed over my lifetime through various avenues. As one gift emerged a new opportunity allowed me to practice and study the gift. Be faithful and available God is not finished with any of us yet.

Refuse to take on Your own Battle

Refuse to take on your own battle; give it to your Lord. Know that the battle that overwhelms you is an enemy assignment; the Spirit will make intercession for you. Life is a challenge. Challenges build you, grow you and build muscle. They are not designed to overwhelm you and shut you down. You are on the winning side the paved way. Not by your power but by My Spirit *(Zechariah 4:6, NKJV)*. Admit you need help, ask, and accept the help available to you. God's grace is free and undeserved favor.

Growing up I learned, "Don't let them see you cry; suck it up and go on." This rule was my compass for a long time in my life and too many times it created my own loneliness and pain. This type of advice does not come with guidelines, boundaries, or limits and does not really solve anything. When are you able to cry? When do you reach out for the help that you might need? The Holy Spirit has come to help you in your weakness, in your need. My need for The Holy Spirit starts with me acknowledging that He can do all things and I cannot. The Spirit can do the impossible I cannot, my human form limits me. He is a limitless God.

God created us to need Him and the more we resist this the deeper we find ourselves looking to self. The further we sink the more we discover self will never be enough. Discovering The Holy Spirit is about realizing the power and authority available to you through Him. We live in a physical body that has limitations, restrictions, and downright inadequacies. We are physical but the battles we encounter are spiritual. You cannot fight a spiritual battle in the physical. The Holy Spirit is spirit, so no human ingenuity can ever do what The Holy Spirit can and will.

Second Corinthians 12:10 (NKJV) "For when I am weak, He is strong."

First Peter 5:7 (NKJV) "Cast all your care upon Him for He cares for you."

Prayer

You are great and there is no one like You, Creator of heaven and Earth, my beginning, and my end. You are my light in the darkness my salvation in my destruction. You are always available to me, and I know that without You I can do nothing. I come boldly before Your throne for Your grace, mercy and help in this time of need. Do what only You can do; I give my greatest concerns over to You. In Your Name, Amen

What do I do when I am weak? I call on my Father. He is strong.

Spiritual Battles are Not Physical

His Spirit gives us power. Years ago, I was a middle school teacher. In one of my five classes I had forty-five, eighth grade, thirteen-year-olds in a crowded classroom. The room was so crowded that I even had kids at my desk. Despite the crowdedness of the class, you could hear a pin drop in there. We had to endure- a crowded classroom, textbooks mildewed together, no photocopies for anyone (the copy room shut down and bolted closed), and the stench of mold and dust emitted from a massive air conditioning system. I spent my early teaching days in that school. My battles were not the conditions of my classroom or the level of my students. My battles were in the spirit where no physical hand would ever touch. I spent my class preparation in prayer, preparing for the battle, being in the battle, and winning the battle with persistent prayer. I prayed persistently before school, in school and in my car for my students, my sanity, the families, and the school. The problems in the community flooded the school; from lockdowns due to a person on campus with a gun to eighth grade drug dealers selling at lunch. Parents only came to school if their child got a detention not for a class failure.

As I herded my kids each day into my classroom, I was parent, teacher, police officer, and even counselor. My kids transformed as they walked through the threshold, a calm came over them. Even if my day ran into problems, my students would confess their crimes to me without me ever asking and sometimes my most trying kids moved or transferred out of my class or school Before my eyes, I saw transformations occur in that classroom. From the class skipper who never missed class to the genius who tutored her friends, they all came to my class. Trust the spirit for direction, the victory. Do not let the physical evidence distract you. Do not believe the accusations or lies designed to destroy you. Distractions make you look at the limitations, the people, the job, the lack, and keep you there. Refuse to trust in the physical obstacles. Do not camp out at the side of the road.

My coworkers always teased me that I had an invisible bat because the same bad kids that were terrors in their class, never gave me any trouble. As a teacher I could do absolutely nothing about bad kids. My students would be in trouble all over the school building or put out of the school for disciplinary problems. My dependence on the spirit kept me. Trust the spirit in your weakness. Some days I found myself in the principal's office professing how I wanted to quit, while plotting my exit he would encourage me to give it another chance. The Spirit never failed to give me new power, strategy, or weapons for the constant struggle. I cried, prayed, and trusted the spirit would lead me to do even what was contrary to my knowledge. In my greatest weakness He never left me alone. Every day I grew in spirit and the experience transformed me to know that my strength would be replenished at the dawn of the new day.

> *John 16:33 (NKJV) "These things I have spoken to you, that in me you may have peace. In the world you will have tribulation; but be of good cheer, I have overcome the world."*

> ### Prayer
>
> *All power and authority given to me through The Father. Every need that I have I give to You. The needs I know and the needs I do not know You supply them all. I call to You. Great and mighty are you. I know You hear my requests, and You will answer all that I need in all my circumstances. Amen.*

How do I have strength to fight a spiritual battle?
Through The Spirit of God who intercedes for me.

Collaborate with Divine Creativity

Collaborate with The Holy Spirit for your creative inspirations. Our own imaginations limit us. If we can imagine it, we can believe it to be so. The Word tells me God can do above all I ask or think according to the power (of my faith) that works in me *(Ephesians 3:20, NKJV)*. God is the source of creativity. When The Spirit of God stepped into the universe, *"The Earth was without form, and void; and darkness was on the face of the deep. And The Spirit of God was hovering over the face of the waters,"* (Genesis 1:2, NKJV). God's creativity can be seen in us, His creation, and the universe.

The limiting control of your own imagination will stop the creativity that The Holy Spirit can move in you. The Spirit calls us to collaborate with Him in a relationship to create and flow in His imagination, which is who we are. From the very beginning when God created us, He created us in His image that means we can do what He can do. *"So, God created man in His own image; in the image of God, He created him; male and female He created them,"*

(Genesis 1:27, NKJV). Our collaboration with the Holy Spirit allows our creative abilities to be explosive and move beyond our imaginations.

Our part is to cultivate a relationship with the spirit in our lives. Dedicate and commit your gifts and talents to God and your purpose. God knows our potential even if we are not convinced and He is waiting to partner with you. Countless people in history (and today) record that their inspirations have come from God. These include the Katherine Johnson, Isaac Newton, William Tyndale, and Gary Starkweather's. Think Biblically, Godly, about your work, what you put your hand to do and collaborate with the spirit. I, for example, am a teacher by calling and my work provides a means to teach all kinds of people. When I am teaching or planning my classes God shows me how to orchestrate a lesson, gives me creative ideas, answers to topics or how to address students on a topic. I collaborate with the spirit. My lessons and classes have been recognized as exemplary while my students have scored highly on state standards and achievements. My students always recognize that my class challenges them in a way they have never experienced. I could never have achieved the successes I have obtained without The Spirit. *"... and He has filled him with The Spirit of God, in wisdom and understanding, in knowledge and all manner of workmanship, to design artistic works, to work in gold and silver and bronze..." (Exodus 35:31-32, NKJV).*

> *Second Corinthians 3:18 (NASB) "And we all, who with unveiled faces contemplate the Lord's glory, are being transformed into his image with ever-increasing glory, which comes from the Lord, who is the spirit."*

> ### Prayer
>
> *Father of the universe, Creator God of wonders. You are God and there is no one like You. You have given me all my gifts and talents to serve You and Your people. My gifts are not my own. Today I commit to partner with You, to learn how I can grow with the gifts You have given me. Show me the way that I should go. Guide my hands and feet. I pray for Your divine wisdom as I commit to becoming all that You designed for me to be. In Your Name, Amen.*

How do I create like My Creator? I develop my relationship with The Holy Spirit.

The very first scripture in The Bible reflects the creativity of The Holy Spirit, "*God created the heavens and the Earth,*" (Genesis 1:1, NKJV). "*God created man in his own image,*" (Genesis 1:27, NKJV). We are creators. We can create all kinds of things and we continue to create inventions and clever devices that have yet to be discovered. We can foster our creativity by nurturing our abilities and developing our relationship with The Holy Spirit, The Original Creator. In Christ we are new creations *(Second Corinthians 5:17, NIV)*. As a new creation we are called to renew our minds and not conform to the patterns of this world *(Romans 12:2, NIV)*. Renewing our minds requires us to know the mind of Christ by committing to reading The Word and allowing our mind to apply The Word and The Spirit into our life. It is through God's grace that we can operate in our different gifts *(Romans 12:6, NIV)*. I am given the gifts, but it is The Spirit operating in my life that allows for the transformation. The Spirit operating in my life allows me to do good works, even greater works than my Father *(John 14:8-12, NIV)*. I am filled with wisdom, understanding, knowledge and all kinds of skills to make artistic designs by The Spirit of God *(Exodus 35:31, NIV)*. It is The Holy Spirit that provides the skill for us to do all kinds of work that we do *(Exodus 35:35, NIV)*.

If You Can Think It Then It Can Be

Most of us do not identify with being creative. We might even say, "Oh I am not the creative type, artsy, that's not really me." If you are a child of God and God is your Creator, then you are inherently creative. Critical thinking, problem solving, imagining, creating, forming, and making are part of the creative process. As a teacher of gifted students, I develop and assess a student's gifted ability and potential. In the gifted class I foster student's giftedness by creating tasks to identify skills and interests, which are then developed with practice over time. Students' giftedness in a particular subject is a natural ability. In the classroom instruction, assignments are designed to further develop this ability through challenging exercises to replicate the skills by then applying those new skills to create a new product. Students apply, replicate, and create. Soon the creation has doubled and with more time and practice year after year there are inventions, witty problems with solutions, and the most unimaginable creations. Students in an English classroom will produce stories, poetry, and even books. Some of the students will engage in contests on state and national levels. There are original dramas written by students and performances created by the gifted English student. Every student works to develop their giftedness focusing on refining their ability from exemplary to mastery.

As a creative soul there have been opportunities to develop my relationship with The Holy Spirit to create. One year I represented my school at a sister school in another country. As part of this international exchange program, I had to take five students with me for a month. Although The Holy Spirit had prompted me to agree to the task, I really did not know how to go about any of the tasks ahead of me. The more I learned about the exchange the more I knew I was really having to create things I knew nothing about. From selecting the five ordained students out of five hundred, to leading my Azeri host's husband to The Gospel on Easter Sunday. I was able to go across a foreign nation with the collaboration of The Spirit to help my students get research from scientists, researchers, ambassadors, and librarians in the country. My host kept asking how I told the taxi drivers where to go. How did you find out the answer to the questions? There was a close connection that I developed with The Spirit and the more I trusted The Spirit for the source of my creations the more I had. The list went on and on. This experience was life changing and the fruit of the prayer I had kept glued to my lips, "Oh God I want to do all that you want me to do. I want to pass this test and bring The Word to this nation." The opportunity to go to an unreached nation such as Azerbaijan and to plant even a seed of The Gospel was bigger than anything I could ever plan. I never imagined I could ever return to the country and my urgency to get The Word out burned in my heart. As a side note, my true desire to go to this country was to bring The Gospel to a Muslim nation. This country is in The 10/40 Window. From my missionary knowledge, countries in The 10/40 Window, is where the majority of the world's Muslims, Hindus, and Buddhists reside. It has historically been considered an area of unreached people groups. This window is located in the rectangular area of North Africa, the Middle East and

Asia about ten degrees north and forty degrees north latitude. As a missionary it was important for me to be there and share The Gospel.

You limit your creativity, The Creator does not. All of us are creative because we inherit this from The Father. There are inventions and creations that are waiting for you to discover and to solve them; so, get beyond yourself and collaborate with The Spirit. Let me share how creativity works. First you will need to do your own work. Do your homework, study your gift, meditate on the possibilities, and invite the spirit for divine inspiration. Remember how I said that as the gifted teacher I create opportunities to develop giftedness. The Holy Spirit does the same for you. He creates the opportunities and like a good teacher He looks to develop the potential you have inside; you can trust Him. God does not give up on us; He will not just let you pass. He knows you. He knows when to plant transformation in your heart.

> *Genesis 1:27 (NKJV) "So, God created man in His own image; in the image of God, He created him."*

> *Romans 12:2 (NKJV) "And do not be conformed to this world, but be transformed by the renewing of your mind, that you may prove what is that good and acceptable and perfect will of God."*

> *Revelation 4:11 (NKJV) "You are worthy, O Lord, to receive glory and honor and power; For You created all things, And by Your will they exist and were created."*

> **Prayer**
>
> *I cannot do any of this life, but I trust in You. I pray for the understanding I need to decipher, decode the situation at hand. I am praying for understanding, newfound gadgets, and inventions. Let my eyes expand to encompass all of You. Engulf me in Your glory. Show me Your way; enlighten my path in new ways, Your ways and not my own. I reject the old and embrace the new.*
> *In Your Name, Amen*

How can I create the new and the unfound solutions of my life? By asking, listening, and moving as The Spirit guides.

Key THREE
Move in Faith

Move in faith and act. Faith is the evidence of things not seen, so if I move in what I know for sure or in what I have logically figured out that is not faith that is my logic, ingenuity, know how in the situation. Faith is not determined by how much I have. No faith is moving, acting on the power of my belief in what God can do, not what I already know can happen.

Your relationship with God determines your threshold of faith. In Matthew 18:1, the disciples, the followers of Christ, wanted to know how to become great in The Kingdom. Jesus answered them by bringing a child into the discussion stating, *"…become, like children [trusting, humble, and forgiving], you will never enter the Kingdom of heaven,"* (Matthew 18:3, AMP). Have you ever been around a child? A child is trusting because they believe in you. A child does not ask you for the evidence of what you say will happen or not. They do not think about what happened last year when they did not get to go to the park or something. They hold to what you say as truth and expect for it to happen. They do not keep asking for what you have promised. I have always been careful what I say to my children whether it be a wish or a plan because they remember and most importantly, they expect it to happen. Children can dream and imagine and none of it has to do with a spiritual maturity; that is what faith is all about.

Moving in faith is moving even when I don't see evidence of something. Faith even believes in the unknown or the unimagined outcome. This is a difficult step to take but it is necessary. The beauty of moving in faith is that it increases your confidence and gives you the proof of God's closeness and authenticity. You will always be able to look back on how God did what He did in a time before.

Hebrews 11:1 (NKJV) "Now faith is the substance of things hoped for, the evidence of things not seen. For by it the elders obtained a good testimony."

Matthew 17:20 (NKJV) "If I have the faith of a mustard seed, then I can tell this mountain to move, and it will. "

Deuteronomy 7:9 (NKJV) "Therefore, know that the Lord your God, He is God, the faithful God who keeps covenant and mercy for a thousand generations with those who love Him and keep His commandments."

Prayer

I pray today Lord give me the faith that I need to believe the impossible. Increase my faith even in my everyday situations. I know that You are faithful, and I can trust You. My willingness to act on my faith daily strengthens my commitment to move in faith. I breakdown any and every obstacle that would distract me from the prize of faith You have for me.
Amen

How do I grow in my faith? By exercising my faith in the everyday.

I pray every day because I never know what a day will bring in a school building. Any day, any moment, a potential problem can arise with a student, parent, administrator, the district, and even shooters. No matter what can be scheduled, school is not a controlled environment for a teacher. So, I have to always pray. I recall a problem arose on the last day before the end of the school year. During the year children were absent either from sickness or disinterest and parents were disconnected and angry. But in the last week of school those same families suddenly come to life. Well before the close of school a student decided she wanted a better grade, and I was going to be the one to give it to her. My grades at that time had been closed and finished, so I was surprised about the request. The one inquiry from the student quickly escalated to the principal and a full-scale investigation, and coercion by the administration. What was I to do besides my usual clarification and explanation of a grade that had been noted two weeks prior? I sat at my desk praying, asking the Lord for the direction to end this sudden battle. I listened and waited. As I sat maintaining an outward composure, I was thoroughly annoyed as I tried to navigate a classroom of students and the barrage of emails between the parent and the office. The Lord gave me some directions to take in the situation. I was starting to feel the heat to say the least. I heard the student discussing with another student (in another language) that I knew the demands she was going to get because she had called her mother. I kept praying as I reviewed the assignment, to adjust the weight of the assignment for the whole class. I put in a call to the union representative for the parent meeting. Even with the changes, the student's overall grade was the same, but the assignment grade looked better. Later that day after class my administrator talked to me about the choices I needed to make and the consequences I could encounter in the process. I kept thinking all of this because a student wants a better grade! There was no discussion about their lack of completing the assignment well. In faith before the final meeting, I made the last move the Lord gave me, read the warning from my principal about what the outcome needs to be, and waited to meet with my administrator and the parent. In the meeting both the parent and child were speechless. The student was reprimanded by the administrator for waiting until the last day of school to improve the grade. I could only give God the glory for the complete turnaround. This is one of so many God interventions over the course of my years as a teacher. No day can ever be a day without prayer. I am always reminded of *Deuteronomy 31:8, (NKJV)*, *"And the Lord, He is the One who goes before you. He will be with you; He will not leave you nor forsake you; do not fear nor be dismayed."*

Faith is a daily exercise. As a teacher I am reminded every day that I can do nothing in my own power. Praying first, trusting God, and most often leaving it in God's hands. At times God may give you actionable steps for the situation.

Faith, We Need It

Faith is not something you can touch, but you can see it all around you. Without faith it is impossible to please God *(Hebrews 11:6, NIV)*. Faith is about trusting God and not yourself. When I was growing up faith was not a discussed topic, but we all knew it existed and thrived in our lives. We had evidence that faith worked, so you just had to believe. There were those witnesses of my mother's cancer diagnosis and her testament of healing each time. My grandmother's proclamation of how she defeated the doctor's prognosis of a crippling disease and was not only walking but dancing to the Lord. Then there were those church testimonies every Sunday that shared the impossible faith of provision, healing, and employment the Lord provided always right on time. Hearing all those testimonies one could only be a believer. I remember wondering what am I to believe in? Did just believing hard enough make something happen? Sometimes, when things did not happen for the people around me, I wondered what did they not believe? Did they fail in their believing? Time would eventually give me my own personal opportunity to have faith and believe.

The first time I can really remember understanding about God's power and faithfulness I was around six. I was sitting in the front seat of my mother's station wagon and my sister was in the back seat. We were on the way to school. In those days seat belts were not required and no one worried about using them. My mom was driving, and the morning was foggy and rainy the kind where you can't see too far ahead. My mom stopped at the stop sign and waited. Out of nowhere a car hit us in a head on collusion. My head went straight to the windshield that shattered and I folded on the dashboard unconscious. My mother grabbed me and called my name a couple of times to wake me up. With the windshield shattered and no seat belt it was a miracle I had not gone through the window at the speed the car had been hit. My only injury was a bump on my forehead. My family always believed God never failed. His faithfulness to us supersedes anything we could ever imagine. My grandmother would often say, "God is a miracle working God."

Another crucial time for me happened when I was fourteen, I developed a cyst in one of my breasts. One breast was significantly larger and painful. It was so painful I could not even wear any brassiere. I tried all I knew to not share my pain because I was scheduled to go on a cross country trip to California and I did not want to miss going for the summer. When my breast looked the size of a small melon, and I couldn't even wear a closed shirt. At that point I told my mother. Her first reaction, when she saw what I was experiencing, went from pain to fear. At that time, she had encountered cancer at least two times and her face said she was very afraid for me. The doctor decided he would use surgery to remove this growing cyst and determine the next steps. I was scheduled for the next appointment to draw out some fluid from the cyst. I was petrified and my imagination went wild in fear. As soon as we got in the car from the doctor my mother wasted no time. She said in a very calm and serious voice before we left the parking lot of the doctor's office, "Either you believe that doctor and let him cut on you or God to heal you." I was shocked. There was no sympathy, no crying – her words were matter-of-fact. Then she asked me point blank which was I believing. I knew it was not a question of faith but a statement of faith that was required in my response. I said, "God," in a low guttural voice because I knew that was who would heal me, but I was scared. We never discussed the cyst and that cyst dissolved by the time I returned to the doctor. I had been suffering with that cyst for two months, and in a week, it was gone. The doctor tried to provide a scientific estimation of what had happened, but I knew my whole family and I had prayed, and God healed. I remember thinking God is real and that moment forever changed my life. There is only one God that heals. Since that time, my own faith has been repeatedly tested and my faith in God has only grown stronger. I encourage myself in the Lord of what He has done in times past and continues to do in my life.

We each need a measure (level or amount) of faith. Our faith allows us to grow in our spiritual gifts and it keeps us humbled. We recognize we need God, and our faith is the only thing between us accomplishing all the Lord has given us to do. The scripture *"…everyone who is among you, not to think of himself more highly than he ought to think, but to think soberly, as God has dealt to each one a measure of faith,"* (Romans 12:2-3, NKJV). Without faith, I would only have what I could do, and that would be an extremely limited life. Faith is essential to the life of the believer.

Faith essentials:

1. The law establishes faith *(Romans 3:31, NASB).* In other words, faith upholds the law. You do not have to choose faith over the law. We see the law established in the Old Testament and throughout the Old and New Testament we see acts of faith from the pillars of faith and Jesus.
2. Faith comes by hearing The Word of God *(Romans 10:7, NASB).*
3. Have faith in God *(Mark 11:22, NASB).*
4. From faith-to-faith reveals God's righteousness *(Romans 1:17, NASB).*
5. We walk by faith not by sight *(Second Corinthians 5:7, NASB).*
6. Faith needs works *(James 2:17, NASB).* Without works faith is dead. Faith needs something to show itself through.
7. Faith grows by works *(James 2:18, NASB).* By the works of faith, we have the faith to believe even more. Our faith does not stay a standard size throughout our lives.
8. Faith is a shield extinguishing the fiery darts of the evil one *(James 2:26, NASB).*
9. Ask in faith, do not doubt, believe, receive and you will have them *(Mark 11:24, NASB).*
10. Faith tested gives you endurance *(James 1:3, NASB).*

Romans 12:2-3 (NASB) "...everyone who is among you, not to think of himself more highly than he ought to think, but to think soberly, as God has dealt to each one a measure of faith."

Hebrews 11:6 (NASB) "Without faith it is impossible to please God."

Prayer

Thank You Lord for my measure of faith. Your righteousness has grown my faith. Everything that You have given me has always shown me Your love for me and the truth of who You are. I put all that I ask in Your hands by Your will. You are faithful and I know that Your faithfulness transcends my time and space. Your Word has proven Your faithfulness to me. Teach me to always reach for You first and trust You above my own beliefs.
In Your Name, Amen

How do I operate in my faith and not fear? By knowing who God is in His Word.

Fear can be paralyzing, and it is the number one tactic the enemy will use to stop you. Look around you everything that is operating in the physical realm from our health to our safety operates from the platform of fear. The worst fear by far is the fear we propagate in our own minds and feed with uncontrolled thoughts. Fear is real, so I am not going to say ignore it, move on, and get going. What I will say is we do not have to live in a place of fear and never obtain the life God has for you.

Knowing who God is will definitely move you pass the fear you are experiencing. In *Psalms 27:1-3 (NLT)* The Word says, *"The Lord is my light and salvation-so why should I be afraid? The Lord is my fortress protecting me from danger, so why should I tremble?... when my enemies and foes attack me, they will stumble and fall. Even when I am attacked, I will remain confident."* It is knowing who God is against the fear you are facing that will get you moving pass your fear. I cannot tell you all the fears I have faced in my own personal life. But those fears have run from financial ruin to the safety of the lives of my children and myself from a disturbed neighbor. Added to those were the fears in my professional life, which include a state of constant threat of livelihood, safety, accusations, and disrespect. Those fears have been with me for the last thirty years. Fear is real but knowing nothing I face is bigger than God, reminding myself that the enemies will fall, and yet God remains the same for me in all of it. I have held onto that Word over and over, reminding myself of the testimonies of my life to overcome the fear.

My father always loved quoting advice of famous people. General Patton was always his favorite. General Patton said, "There is a time to take counsel of your fears, and there is a time to never listen to any fear." My father's all-time favorite quote was, "Nothing beats a failure but a try." So, from a child fear was never a viable option for me. I have done many things in fear and most of the time it has allowed me to depend more on God and not myself. One of my favorite scriptures is *Matthew 12:20, NASB, "A bruised reed He will not break..."* Sometimes we are more fragile because we are more afraid of the failure. Remember who God is and encourage yourself by reading what He has done in times past.

This is my Testimony

The Law of Faith requires us to believe in God without doubting. For a person to be saved they must first acknowledge that God is the savior of mankind that is their first step of faith. Believing God exists or believing in the God that created this Earth is not the same as salvation. Our salvation is a gift of God *(Ephesians 2:8, NLT)*. In *Mark 11:22-25 (NLT)* Jesus taught the Law of Faith as —speaking, believing, receiving, and forgiving. The Law of Faith is based on Jesus not on you. Once you speak in faith; faith begins to work. Have faith in God, not your doubts. When you pray, forgive anything you have against anyone. Forgiveness is necessary for faith to work *(Mark 11:25-26, NLT)*. The testimony of faith is a truth, law, or evidence given by a witness for the purpose of sharing a lesson learned from God. Throughout The Bible we can see the testimony of faith given by many witnesses of the lessons they learned about faith. As I have said, faith is believing in God and every testimony is a testament of God to that believer and other listeners of the story. Each testimony builds your faith and others in the process.

My testimonies of faith encourage me in the Lord. Each one that I have encountered has moved my faith deeper in the Lord, while at the same time The Word is demonstrated in my life. Each testimony is a 'stone of remembrance' for me. Let me share one of my testimonies of faith to show you how this works, and let it serve as an encouragement for you.

After a bedridden pregnancy filled with weekly sonograms, preterm labor, and little weight gain I gave birth to my second daughter. Even down to her birth there seemed to be unusual medical concerns-early term birth, induced labor, and still she was born 24 hours later. Though a small, lightweight baby, we still got to go home on time. Once we got home, we began to run into a new set of problems. The baby could not keep any of the prescribed formulas down. My small, petite girl daily was slowly losing her few birth pounds. As we went back and forth to the doctor trying to find a good formula, my beautiful girl seemed to be slipping away from us right before our eyes. After going to the doctor for the fourth time in one week the doctor admitted my dehydrated and listless daughter. Ambulanced to the hospital the medic could not even feed a vein in her now flat veins. The only viable option was in her stomach as the medic struggled to keep her alive on the way to the hospital.

For a week doctors ran tests, changed her formulas, and still her body was not responding; she was slipping away more. I remember the day I sat holding her listless body in my arms. At that point she was not even crying and honestly her doctor did not have a next move. In that hospital room that night I prayed to God, or should I say I asked God, "You brought her here to take her away? Why would you give me this baby to leave me?" That is all I said, and, in my heart, I knew He wanted her to stay not go back home to Him. From the beginning of my pregnancy to that day we had encountered problem after problem trying to get her to this Earth, healthy and whole. The next day the doctor had a prognosis. My baby went home on permanent medication required every four hours and was assigned a kidney specialist.

When we went home, and her care routine set in, the Lord spoke to me yet again and promised she would never start school on the medication. She was three months old at that time, and I held onto that word for two years. No one was on my side, only God. My well-meaning Bible group abandoned me and said I lacked faith to trust God by holding onto the medication. I held onto my promise from God for her healing. Years later her doctor made a brave step forward and took her off the medicine temporarily. I had spent two years of expensive specialist visits, medications, special formulas, and well-meaning friends constantly badgering me to move in faith and take her off the medicine. Their words, "prove that God heals," but there was more to my test. There was nothing to prove. God does heal. I knew what God had said to me and I knew He kept His promises. Her kidney doctor had told me one time my daughter was the only patient that he had treated that never had a kidney removed to recover. When the doctor took her off the medicine for a few days to see how she would do she never went back. I trusted in God even if it was a lonely journey. God always keeps His Word, and He does heal all kinds of sicknesses; that is my testimony of faith.

Romans 10:17 (NKJV) "So then faith comes by hearing, and hearing by the word of God."

Deuteronomy 7:9 (NKJV) "Therefore know that the Lord your God, He is God, the faithful God who keeps covenant and mercy for a thousand generations with those who love Him and keep His commandments."

Prayer

Faith comes by hearing. Thank You, God for all that You have promised to me. God I am listening to Your words. You are always faithful and true. May I always be obedient to Your Word and never doubt what You have spoken. I am so honored that You have chosen me to share Your deepest thoughts and desires for me.
Amen.

***How do I keep my faith in the crowd*?** Recognize the only voice that is faithful and true. His name is Father.

Fuel for Faith

What fuels our faith? There are some elements that can keep our faith fueled. Once God gives the promise, we will invariably look at the impossibilities of it happening. We can see there are limitations of the promise while looking through our circumstance or perspective. My limitations included: the results of the medical tests of my daughter's kidneys; the doctors had no answers; no cure and taking medication every four hours. Our faith is not in us, the situation, or even the doctor, but in the faithfulness and healing power of God. *"For the promise that he would be the heir of the world was not to Abraham or to his seed through the law, but through the righteousness of faith,"* (Romans 4:13, NKJV). So, we have to see past those limitations and look to God to fulfill the promise. God promised Abraham (formerly known as Abram) that he would be the father of many nations. God made a covenant with Abraham to bless and multiply him *(Genesis 17:1-5, NKJV).* At the time of the promise Abraham had no children. He was 86 years old when he received the promise. Fourteen years later, at 100, Sarah had the promised child. Sarah, old like Abraham, had been barren all those years.

The promise may have a fulfillment time, or an expected arrival time. I had three years before my daughter's healing. Abraham had fourteen years. God is preparing the way, preparing you for the future. This time can vary and there is really no set time, but your position during the wait is to believe the promise and do not look at the limitations. If you look hard enough the list of limitations can keep you up at night, but spend time being open to the preparation God is doing in you for the future promise fulfillment. Look to the God of impossibilities who created the universe. *"In the beginning God created the heavens and the Earth," (Genesis 1:1, NKJV).* He can create the world in less than a week, so He surely can fulfill your promise.

Varying public comment will be evident in the waiting of the promise. Unbelief either propelled by you or well-meaning friends or family stills resolute faith. The witnesses want to see if this God you know is real. Are you real? The commentators show up everywhere in The Word from Noah's ark to the thief on the cross. The public commentators, the witnesses are watching. The Word tells us to lay aside every weight, encumbrance and sin that can entangle us in this is part of the preparation for the promise. Endurance here is the ability to do the will of God during the process, race, so you may receive the promise *(Hebrews 10:36, NKJV). "Therefore, we also, since we are surrounded by so great a cloud of witnesses, let us lay aside every weight, and the sin which so easily ensnares us, and let us run with endurance the race that is set before us," (Hebrews 12:1, NKJV).* Fix your eyes and do not accept any imitations or anything less than the promise. When the doctor gave me the medication for my daughter, I could have stopped there accepting that as the promise of healing, and wholeness. Abraham was forever known as the father of many nations, the exalted father, took 100 years before he even became a father. Fix your eyes firmly on Jesus; do not lose heart in the promise.

Worship is a fuel of faith. When you glorify God, you build up your faith, and fear flees; it has no place. Worship blesses us and The Father. There will be those naysayers trying to remind you of all the impossibilities. Some may even begin to have you question what did God really say? The mockers discourage you and discredit your promise. Give God the glory even before the fulfilled promise.

Spend your time in worship, build your spirit, and dismiss the mockers *(Luke 8:53-54, NKJV)*.

Surrender all the situations and problems to God. Own none of it, less you will surely try to figure it out or worst worry yourself about it. When I was in my graduate leadership classes there was an exercise, we would engage in to assess problems in a scenario and the steps we could follow. The first step was to identify the different stakeholders and match their level of responsibility to the problem. The exercise revealed the owner of each responsibility which gave you a better perspective on the situation, thus possibly eliminating burnout and micromanaging which can easily befall a leader. I enjoyed this exercise because it made you realize you cannot solely own the problem when there are other stakeholders responsible for it. God is solely able to perform any promise He has made, and we have no responsibility to make it happen. It is tempting to try to take it on, but our efforts can be costly. Abraham tried to make it happen in his way with Hagar. Our efforts can be detrimental and costly a price to be paid for you and future generations.

Remember what you have believed in to be a believer- the Resurrection, Jesus is God, and Jesus Christ forgiving your sins. In comparison it is small to believe victory over whatever you are facing. Sometimes when I think about what I can worry about I have to smile because in the big picture it is minuscule in comparison to how great God is.

> *Romans 4:20 (NKJV) "He did not waver at the promise of God through unbelief, but was strengthened in faith, giving glory to God."*

> *Romans 4:21 (NKJV) "...and being fully convinced that what He had promised He was also able to perform."*

Hebrews 11:3 (NKJV) "By faith we understand that the [c]worlds were framed by the word of God, so that the things which are seen were not made of things which are visible."

Prayer

My Father, my Provider, my God, Faithful One there is no God like You. Savior of my soul, Creator of the universe, I give You the glory over all the promises You have given me. Thank You for caring for every detail of my life and this day my faith is in You aligned with Your will in my situation to do only what You can do for me. Thank You.
Amen

How do I hold onto the promise? God is able. Give Him the glory

God Always Makes Provision

God's provision is not limited to bank accounts, checks, credit scores or paychecks. God's provision is boundless and encompassing. David says in The Word, *"The Lord is my shepherd; I shall not want...My cup overflows... Surely goodness and loving kindness will follow me all the days of my life..."* (Psalm 23:1-6, NASB). Where does your belief in God's provision begin or even end? My start I can say began at home with my single parent household. It did not matter what we did not have, it mattered more what God could provide. I do not remember any discussions about not having money or if

God would make the provision available, I always knew I would have provision. No, we were not wealthy, but yes, I always knew that God could and would make provision. God gave me all the 90% and I gave him my 10% that is really where it all begins. I can remember tithing ten cents because I had received a dollar for the week, which was real and I never begrudged what I gave to God because I knew in my child's mind, I had the most of it. I never yearned for anything. I can even remember well into my middle school years my sister telling me we were not rich. I was a little dumbfounded by the information. I did not ask her to explain, but if I wasn't wealthy then who was. If I was missing something it was not because we did not have it, yet. I had everything that I not only wanted but needed. I was a content person. I did not ask for much but my belief in provision was simple. When money got tight in our household, I saw my mother give her last dollar to someone she said had a greater need and we could get more of it. I never doubted the provision would be there. My mother had always provided and God, who can supply all my needs, would continue to do the same and more.

God's provision begins again in what we believe. What we believe about God and the kind of provision that He provides. Remember provision is not just about money in the bank. Provision is everything we need and things we do not even recognize what we need. When I speak about provision some may think about a camping trip preparing the provisions; others may think a means to accomplish or a need beyond the scope of humankind. Provision in The Bible refers to supply. God's provision covers the body (physical), soul (mind, intellect, will, and emotion), and the spirit(eternal) of a person. For me God's provision has come in the physical- a car, job, at the same time provision has come for a loss, encouragement, and a spiritual need. Does your provision stop at the physical what you can see or believe? Does it fall short of what God wants for you or your needs? Do I see the provision of God as an earthbound means when it could in fact be a spiritual investment God is making in me? You will always be bound by two concepts -your own definition of the provision and your faith, belief system.

Romans 12:2 (NASB) "And do not be conformed to this world, but be trans-formed by the renewing of your mind, that you may prove what is that good and acceptable and perfect will of God."

Third John 2:2 (NASB) "Beloved, I pray that you may prosper in all things and be in health, just as your soul prospers."

Second Chronicles 20:15 (NKJV) "Listen, all you of Judah and you inhabitants of Jerusalem, and you, King Jehoshaphat! Thus, says the Lord to you: 'Do not be afraid nor dismayed because of this great multitude, for the battle is not yours, but God's.'"

Second Chronicles 20:20 (NKJV) Jehoshaphat stood and said, "Hear me, O Judah and you inhabitants of Jerusalem: Believe in the Lord your God, and you shall be established; believe His prophets, and you shall prosper."

> ### Prayer
>
> *Father all-knowing Father. Ruler of heaven and Earth I only want what You want for me. You have seen me not just today but yesterday and in my future. Show me Your way and give me the eyes to see beyond my physical situation to know You are making provisions for me in my every day. Thank You for the provision that You are providing for me in my situation. (Here you can state the situation, the need.) Give me The Word that I will need to move and the faith to trust in You with my future. I know that Your love encompasses and overwhelms me, and Your blessings make me rich. Amen.*

How does God make provisions for me? God's Word and promises for me are for yesterday, today, and tomorrow.

KEY FOUR

Discerning The Time

For in Everything There is a Season, Seed Time, and Harvest

Timing is important in the teaching profession, the time to teach, the time to listen, the time to repeat and the time to reflect. As a teacher I am always having to learn to discern the appropriate time, the right time, weighing out my options, considering the requirements and evaluating the path to follow. In a classroom of learners, the teacher creates the time, but the students will often unknowingly set the pace. One class may get the concept, love it, and run with it, hit all the marks, and move to the next level; while another class may be at a different pace and need more time.

How do I know the appropriate time for my life? How do I move in the correct time for the next thing? As a teacher I have studied and practiced the timing of my lessons to cover the time in my class. I have figured out how long it will take for the instructions, how long I will allow for a class to settle down, or a student to respond to the question. Unbeknownst to the student, the teacher has planned all of this to achieve optimum results every day, every moment. Now it comes naturally to listen and look for the clues that are before me to gauge the pace. God is the same in our lives.

There are seasons in our lives and every season has a requirement.

We all have heard that timing is everything. Now, I do realize that when we say that we may believe in certain laws of the universe or our ability to appropriately enact or incite something to happen at a particular time. It is the result of an action. I have been one to make it happen whatever it may be. I guess many of us can be guilty of making things happen. Sometimes the extreme we may take to make things happen can be to our own ruin. But in this next step I am talking about the timing that God has created and most importantly how God's timing is perfect not our own.

God will always give you the time. Now He is not going to literally say this is your time to grow, or this is your time for promotion, but He will provide the direction, and/or the words of wisdom that encourage and guide you for the time that you are in. Again, you must listen and move into action and do not judge or try to understand the action you are to take.

Thirty-three years ago, when I quit my insurance position and decided to pursue my master's degree, I never planned to be a teacher. While I was home studying, the Lord began prompting me to apply for a teaching position. I had been praying and asking the Lord to reveal to me the steps I should pursue, and teaching was my word. I made a deal with the Lord - since I was not interested in teaching - to apply to only one position. One position moved me into a new career that has spanned more than thirty years. There is a time for everything in our lives. We must not only discern the time of our season but respond to the season we are facing. We cannot plant when it is the dead of the winter neither can we harvest out of season. *Genesis 8:22, NKJV* reads, *"While the Earth remains, seedtime and harvest, cold and heat, winter and summer, and day and night shall not cease."* The Father says trust me because I know the time I have for your beginning and ending. *"For I know the thoughts that I think toward you, says the Lord, thoughts of peace and not of evil, to give you a future and a hope." (Jeremiah 29:11, NKJV).* When God gives you the time for a thing, He has placed it at the right time not just for you, but for all that are part of it. God looks out for everyone included. God's timing has no grief or sorrow. When I move ahead of this time, I can prolong my season or put off the season that is coming.

So, the next step in this journey is examine the time and the season you are in by seeking and waiting on God. There are so many good examples of a person's seasons in The Bible- Joseph, Abraham, and Moses to name a few. Let us look at Joseph; his life is a series of timings. His father gives him a coat of many colors because he is the favorite child. Joseph has a dream and tells his brothers of his dream striking up their ire. He has another dream and shares it with his father. As the result of sharing his dream his brothers plot to get rid of him. The life of the favorite child, shelter and care has just ushered in a new time in his life. Examine his circumstances, his gifts, rewards, and most importantly his response to the present situation. Did he pick that season? Did God? We can't be certain. In every season, from his slavery, jail time, and his move into the palace, a preparation process was necessary to bring him into the next phase of his life.

What is your present season? Are there any red flags or messages God has sent you in your dreams? Look for patterns in your conversations, situations, or feelings. Currently, is there anything that vaguely resembles a time before? Go before God, seek Him and watch for an answer. If we do not ask our Father, then we can never know how to discern the time. Examine what has been going on around you. Embracing the time is important, but if we ignore it, that could mean a do over. I want to be where God is because that is where the blessing is.

> *Ecclesiastes 8:5 (NKJV) "A wise man's heart discerns both time and judgment Because for every matter there is time and judgment."*

> *Jeremiah 8:7 (NKJV) "Even the stork in the heavens, knows her appointed times; And the turtledove, the swift, and the swallow observe the time of their coming."*

Prayer

Thank You, Lord, for Your seasons that You have created on this Earth. You even the world at a certain time. The natural world is a testimony that everything has a time and season. God, I do not want to miss my season with You. Show me the time that I am in, direct my paths, guide my eyes, lead my heart, so I can be in tune with the season that You have given me to accomplish the tasks that You have for me. I pray for Your directions in everything that I say and do. God give me the season, so I can appropriately apply the wisdom that I need at this time.
Amen.

How can I be wise? It is by wisdom from the Lord.

Hearing from God

In order to hear from God, we have to first discern, recognize, God's voice from any other voice. Discernment means that you can hear, understand The Word spoken to you, and make a judgment for next steps. Discernment starts with wanting to hear from God. The Word says, *"So that you incline your ear to wisdom, and apply your heart to understanding, yes if you cry out for discernment and lift your voice for understanding," (Proverbs 2:3-5, NKJV).* Wanting to hear from God is the same as asking your friend for their honest opinion. Your friend knows if you are sincere, which will determine how much they will share with you. God knows you better than you know yourself. He knows the ones who will listen to His voice. You can fool yourself, but you have little chance of fooling God, your Creator.

My sheep know my voice. Sometimes you wonder is that God? Is that me? Know that in every part of your life God is speaking. Are you listening? Invite God to speak into your life. God's voice lines up with the scripture, The Word of God. There have been times when I have heard a word and it resounded with my spirit. I could not seem to shake what was planted in my spirit and that word would seem to hunt me down. It would show up on the radio, in a conversation, on a TV show confirming and reaffirming God's Word to me repeatedly. God will always agree with His Word. Learn to listen.

Listening is an assessable skill. What does your listening score look like? In the years I have been a second language teacher listening skills have been part of a person's language skills. Ask any reading teacher and they will tell you a student's listening determines their comprehension skills. Listening is different from hearing. One requires cognitive skills and the other the physical functioning of your ears. So, when we hear from God, we must actively listen to engage or act on the message, which is comprehension.

Years ago, I was in my kitchen cleaning and praying, communicating with God. After the birth of my third daughter, I noticed that my once comfortable two-bedroom condominium was getting crowded and overrun with baby toys and items. I remember I was thanking God for His provision, the place that we owned, and the new baby He had given us. Then I heard God say to me, "Ask." Immediately in the spirit I knew He was talking about our house situation. I began to say to the Lord, "I have a home," and I never thought of asking for one because some people are homeless. I felt their need was greater or more necessary. Again, God said for me to, "Ask." I stopped my own excuses and asked the Lord for a home. I had no stipulations except that it would be a place that my husband and I could both agree on. That prayer began the clock on the home that God was giving me. In the process He gave me instructions that made no sense to me many times but again I actively engaged in the process despite me. No one could discourage me, take from me, or destroy what God had given me even when they tried. As He has said I gave you the home so despite the housing crisis, financial upsets in the economy, marriage dissolution, single income, college tuitions, and the pandemic God has kept me in a house that He gave me over twenty-three years ago despite me. So, learn to listen, discern the promise, and do whatever God is asking of you despite you.

Job 9:16 (NKJV) "If I called and He answered me, I would not believe that He was listening to my voice."

Proverbs 19:27 (NKJV) "Cease listening to instruction, my son, and you will stray from the words of knowledge."

James 1:19 (NKJV) "So then, my beloved brethren, let every man be swift to hear, slow to speak, slow to wrath."

Prayer

Thank You, Lord, for always being there for me and listening to my every need. You have listened to me in all my seasons of life. I know that You are there for me. I commit to listening to You. Your words are powerful and true to guide and direct my life. Open my ears and my heart. May Your words penetrate my heart and mind. Speak plainly to me so I may do what You have asked and gain what You have for me.
Amen.

How do I know the path to take? God will direct my path along the way.

Get Your Appointed Time

The Lord's time is not our time. The Lord does not see time as we see it in years, days of the week, morning and evening, and incremental minutes. Time is limitless. The Word says, *"A day to God is a thousand years,"* (*Second Peter 3:8, NASB*). We look at God through our human form on this Earth. We limit the span of time that God creates, and we try very desperately to put God in a box. Now I know this concept is hard to really grasp or figure out through our humanness, but the appointed time God has for everything is not the definition of time we may be thinking. When God told Abraham, he would be the father of many nations, Abraham had no children. *Genesis 18:14, NASB says, "Is anything too hard for the Lord? At the appointed time I will return to you, according to the time of life, and Sarah shall have a son."*

In his waiting Abraham was human. He reminded himself of how old he and his wife Sarah were and figured, "let me see if I can make this happen." Have you ever tried to make it happen in your own strength? I am guilty of doing this; I like to get things going. There is a cost in pushing things along before the appointed time. Sometimes it may delay your future or give you even bigger problems to contend with. I do know from my own experiences of moving ahead of God there is something to pay for our own impatience. Because even though I know God, I have dishonored Him by putting my plans before what He has planned. When I have done this, I am saying I know better than God, my Creator. It is difficult to make a comeback from impatience and moving out of God's timing; some damage may remain. Waiting for God's appointed time produces abundance, fruit, and joy. What God has for us is not necessarily easy, but there is no sorrow in it *(Proverbs 10:22, NASB)*.

So, let us get to knowing this appointed time. Here are steps to be mindful of when you have decided this is that time:

Step 1: You will begin trying to logically figure out how is God going to do something. This is the first sign of you entertaining false imaginations. Your mind starts to get busy, preoccupied with how to make this plan work. The scripture warns us about these vain imaginations. *Romans 1:21 (NJKV), says "...because, although they knew God, they did not glorify Him as God, nor were thankful, but became futile in their thoughts, and their foolish hearts were darkened."* Stop right here, hold your thoughts captive, surrender to God's will and be obedient to His Plan. *Psalm 18:30*

(NKJV) reminds us, *"As for God, His way is perfect; The Word of the Lord is proven; He is a shield to all who trust in Him."* Our heart is deceitful. *Proverbs 16:9, NKJV* tells us that *"A man's heart plans his way, But the Lord directs his steps."*

Step 2: Surrender yourself, trust God, and submit your will. This is when I start praying really for myself and my struggle to submit to the timing of the plan. Some scriptures I like to use to encourage myself include, *Mark 9:23, NKJV, "If you believe all things are possible to him who believes."* Every time my mind starts to entertain a plan, I submit it to God and begin to pray. *Proverbs 19:21, NKJV, "There are many plans in a man's heart, Nevertheless the Lord's counsel—that will stand."* See the enemy, the father of lies, he wants you to believe you cannot wait. God is not doing anything, and you know better. Know your enemy and recognize his scheme to deceive you. *John 10:10, NKJV* says, *"The thief does not come except to steal, and to kill, and to destroy."* No, the enemy does not know the time or plan, but he works to get you to rebel against God to destroy you, the plan, or any future God could have for you.

Step 3: Know that the timing of God is perfect. Silence from God is not an answer but more of a wait, pray. Take the time to seek wise counsel. *Proverbs 1:5, NKJV* reminds us that, *"A wise man will hear and increase learning, and a man of understanding will attain wise counsel."* Listen for the direction, a word, an affirmation to your spirit. Consecrate yourself in prayer, fasting, and waiting for direction. *Proverbs 12:15 NKJV* advises, *"The way of a fool is right in his own eyes, but he who heeds counsel is wise."* Do not get stuck on the time because God's plans are always perfect plans and late is never late with God. God's time is eternity.

Second Peter 3:8 (NKJV) "But, beloved, do not forget this one thing, that with the Lord one day is as a thousand years, and a thousand years as one day."

Genesis 18:14 (NKJV) "Is anything too hard for the Lord? At the appointed time I will return to you, according to the time of life, and Sarah shall have a son."

Romans 1:21 (NKJV) "...because, although they knew God, they did not glorify Him as God, nor were thankful, but became futile in their thoughts, and their foolish hearts were darkened."

Proverbs 16:9 (NKJV) "A man's heart plans his way, But the Lord directs his steps."

Prayer

Our Father who art in heaven hallowed be Thy Name. Thy kingdom come. Thy will be done on Earth as it is in heaven. Lord, I pray for _______________. I submit to Your plans and not my own. You have always loved me even before I even knew You. Guide me, direct my steps only as You are able. Open doors and close doors that need to be closed. Thank You for loving me and always looking out for me. Renew my strength as I wait on You. Amen.

How do I know my appointed time? I trust God and He will direct me.

Watch for The Signs

Seasons announce the days and months of our lives. In Florida, torrential rains that last for days announces summer, flooded yards, walkways, and streets, and then there is the humidity in between. Without even looking at the calendar you know it is June. Some days as the temperatures rise to a breaking point the heat breaks by a sudden shower that is not long, but just enough to cool everything. As the summer sets in there are more days of extreme heat and less and less rainy afternoons. Before you realize it, you are past the 4th of July with the high temperatures of summer. Just like nature, our lives follow a cycle of seasons not as predictable as the four seasons, but they do come with signs. Each season of your life has a significant contribution or turn in your life.

Galatians 4:10 (NKJV) tells us to, "*...observe days and months and seasons and years.*" When we observe we pay attention to everything because we are not sure where the sign is leading. Every day and month are leading to the path the Lord is orchestrating and we do not want to miss any of it. Can the path have twists or turns we do not expect or even want? Yes, because God is always seeking to make us grow, enrich us, and expand the person that we are to the person we can be. Keep in mind The Father knows you in ways you do not. He sees your present but knows your future. What are the prayers, words that God is speaking to your heart? Pay attention because the signs are speaking to you about your season.

No season, no matter how many you experience will be the same. A decree can announce your season.

The decree is an earnest declaration you make from the heart of God. In one season of my life, it began with a word planted in my heart. A simple observation that I professed aloud to just myself. I said, "I don't want to live and die here." I was not really thinking about the idea of leaving before I even said it. This decree propelled my new season.

Once the decreed word hit the atmosphere, I never thought it through but soon after I made this decree, my days and months began to work out this word. Because I had said this decree I began to receive and work with the opportunities and situations that started to unfold. I was open. Then my spouse's job relocated to a state outside of our hometown, even though he had proclaimed he would never leave our state. When the decision to move out of our hometown became urgent for both of us, I put it to prayer. I committed to praying and I did not care how long because I did not want to be any place God was not. I left the decision in God's hands and not my own.

Over the course of the year more details started to unfold some quickly, some miraculously, and many seem now to be incredible. As days led to months all the signs prepared the opportunity to move us out of the state even down to the late-night job interview invitation two days before my future job start date. Aware that I was in a new season- I anticipated the preparation, transformation, and expectation for what was to come.

Since that time of course more seasons have come into my life. None of them have come the same. I am listening for the next steps, praying for situations, meditating on The Word, and waiting when required. If I know who God is, I trust Him with all my life, not just the comfortable part. Sometimes it is not what you might expect or wished in your heart, but I can promise you if you trust God, it would be well. The seasons we encounter require internal changes and spiritual transformations.

The changes are not just happening to me in isolation, they can be transforming for many people involved in the transformation. Spiritual seasons make us face the truth about ourselves and find our own truth.

> *Psalm 90:12 (NKJV) "So teach us to number our days, that we may gain a heart of wisdom."*

> *Genesis 8:22 (NKJV) "While the Earth remains, Seed time and harvest, Cold and heat, Winter and summer, and day and night shall not cease."*

Prayer

Lord, teach me to number my days, so I may gain wisdom for my present and future success. Let me see this season as You do. Open my eyes and my heart to receive the blessings of Your guidance and direction through this time. Make me and shape me in the will You have called me. I do not want to waste any of this time with You. When I go in my own direction direct me back, I commit myself to Your plan. Thank You for loving me enough not to leave me where I am and taking me where I need to be to receive all that You have for me.
Amen.

How can I know the direction of my season? I must be slow to speak, quick to listen and obedient to my directions.

The Way that I Should Go

Many times, the question of which way I should go in this season will arise. I have never been afraid of making a decision. I am naturally gifted to make a comprehensive decision and to follow it through. This is where teaching has always been good for me. I have class rules established for the class the first day class convenes. I share those rules in the class syllabus, the rules, and requirements of the class. When a problem arises in the class there is already in place a rule for that particular problem. I address any problem in the class straight on with the student and follow up with them until well the situation is completed. I don't back down or give up with adversity. Adversity eggs me on. So where one may struggle with the next steps or knowing where God is leading, I do not. I have to actually stop myself when a problem or situation arises because my natural reflex is to get it going, take care of it and get it out of the picture. I am actually more stressed by not doing something than doing something.

I do know that some people prefer not to respond to a situation. Their inaction can fall into trying to ignore the problem or just hoping it will resolve itself. They may respond this way because they are not sure of themselves. This may come from lack of experience, fear of failure, or being hesitant of what God really wants them to do. I am confrontational, to say the least, when it comes to problems or situations in my life. So, my rule of thumb is to pray, meditate on The Word, and get a confirmation. I have a 24-hour rule at least that can be extended if I am not confirmed by the spirit for all my moves even if I am fairly sure of what I need to do. I want the spirit to give me the direction so I will beat myself into submission to wait.

So how am I determining the way that I should go in a season? I am not looking for a fleece or sticking a test out there to get a confirmation. My leading starts with a revelation, from a dream, a word dropped in my spirit or just a revelatory word in scripture. I am looking and listening for The Spirit in my day and not to judge The Word as logical or sane. Instead, I position myself to receive. God's direction is never going to violate His Word, so this is where you want to be a good Bible scholar so you can recognize God's direction from your own. There have been times when my answer wakes me at night to a plan on what to do. Stay in the spirit, *Jeremiah 42:3, NKJV* tells us "...the Lord your God may show us the way in which we should walk and the thing we should do." The Spirit guides us into all truth.

There are those reading this who are thinking that doesn't work for me, I need God to come right here and show me the way. Well, I suppose since The Father does know you, He will be able to reveal that to you as He did for Thomas. Thomas, one of the disciples of Jesus, is famously known as 'Doubting Thomas'. After the resurrection of Christ, the other disciples reported to him they had seen the Lord. Thomas' response to them, *"Unless I see in His hands the print of the nails and put my finger into the print of the nails, and put my hand into His side, I will not believe,"* (John 20:24, NKJV). Christ eight days later came to the disciples again and he addressed Thomas, *"Reach your finger here, and look at My hands; and reach your hand here and put it into My side. Do not be unbelieving, but believing,"* (John 20:27, NKJV). Ask Him and He knows what you need to know to move forward. Once you have the revelation of your direction you must move. Partial obedience is still considered disobedience. Don't be a judge on how this direction will work out just move in the direction the spirit is moving you. Responding to the direction of the spirit will produce more opportunities for the spirit to tell you things.

Ephesians 5:16 (NKJV) "redeeming the time, because the days are evil."

Exodus 18:20 (NKJV) "And you shall teach them the statutes and the laws and show them the way in which they must walk and the work they must do."

Colossians 4:5 (NKJV) "Walk in wisdom toward those who are outside, redeeming the time."

Jeremiah 42:3 (NKJV) "that the Lord your God may show us the way in which we should walk and the thing we should do."

Prayer

Lord, I come to You for direction. You are the all-knowing Father. I need to know the way that I should go in this season. Guide my steps, pave my way to follow You in all that I do. My decisions at this time are in subjection to Your leading and truth. I submit my plans to You, and I receive Your wisdom above anyone. My desire is to please You in my life in every aspect of my life.
Amen.

How do I know when to move? Today I hear His voice and I will follow.

Opportunities Only Come Once

Opportunities have an expiration date. Opportunities have a start and an end of term date. Granted you can find another opportunity, who knows maybe better or equal, but it will not be the same opportunity. On my classroom door I have a sign that says, "When opportunity knocks answer the door." There is a physical and spiritual door to opportunity. Physically I have to answer the call, put in the application, reach out, and apply. Spiritually I have to commit on a spiritual, emotional level. *Matthew 10:38, NKJV* says, *"Whoever does not take up their cross and follow me is not worthy of me."* There has been over the last couple of years a focus on right thinking, your mind must sort of be reprogrammed before you can make a physical change. The Word calls it out in *Second Corinthians 10:5 (NIV), "We demolish arguments and every pretension that sets itself up against the knowledge of God, and we take captive every thought to make it obedient to Christ."* You are what you think you are, which will inhibit who you can become. See you can have all the degrees, certifications, friend connections, and know your gift but if your mind has determined I can't do this or that it is beyond my reach, then guess what you will not be ready for the opportunity.

What is an opportunity? It is a chance, an experience, a connection, a risk, or all of them. I look for opportunities and search them out. I invest in looking for opportunities because they have an expiration date and time is ticking. Now some may believe well shouldn't I just wait for the opportunity to find me? Sometimes it will through a connection or referral but note you were looking for that to happen. There will be times your voice will have to be known of your interest or desire. In *Luke 14:27 (NLT)*, Jesus lets us know that a true disciple must first commit spiritually, carry their cross, to follow.

When I am teaching in a class, I try really hard to refrain from being what we call a talking head. Talking and talking while students sit there halfway listening, disengaged. In class I am presenting the information, providing the connection through personal anecdotes, stories and then above all else I am looking for the opportunity to draw a student into the conversation. I am looking to see the connection in their eyes and spirit to release the assignment offer the possibilities and take questions. I may be talking my little spiel, but my mind is working overtime scanning the room, connecting with hearts, and mind to see who is ready for the leap. I will move to that opportunity as a springboard to further explain, answer some questions that have been ruminating in the minds of my students or I may use that opportunity as a connection to another part of the lesson. *Proverbs 27:17 (NASB)* illustrates that, *"As iron sharpens iron, so one person sharpens another."* Opportunities are key to living and thriving, growing, and developing in this Earthly life.

Skills acquired die on their feet if you don't seek to apply them. As a teacher part of our lesson calls for application of the new skill. For a person to have ownership of a skill they must have nonthreatening opportunities to apply that skill. Eventually through this application a student can not only understand but reinvent the skill in different formats, create. When I learn a new skill, my goal is to always use it. Remember that expression use it or lose it. I take that seriously. Opportunities become dividends on your skill investment.

When an opportunity is posted check it out. Ask questions, reach out, because sometimes it maybe that you will need to gather information before you make that leap. Years ago, my school system was offering national certification. When it was first advertised it required a $5,000 dollar investment. Well, I was looking to get an increase in my salary, but I did not want to pay for a degree or any out-of-pocket certifications, so I looked into the program, collected my notes, asked questions, and then tabled it. About a year later the school system decided they had to make an investment, so they decided to pay for the application process and provide a one-time bonus of 10,000 dollars for a teacher who achieved the certification. A year later, I was interested. I was the only teacher in my school applying and I was ecstatic about the opportunity. I received the certification that I still hold today. I got the bonus and for ten years I got an additional bonus yearly of four thousand dollars on top of my salary and raises. I made the investment of time and energy, but I paid no monetary payment. Today this program is not even available in my school system, but I am regularly sought out for jobs and paid committee positions eighteen years later. I have had opportunities because I was willing to physically reach for it; spiritually I invest my gift. I position myself to give to the teaching profession by serving as a mentor for future teachers and students.

Second Corinthians 10:5 (NKJV) "We demolish arguments and every pretension that sets itself up against the knowledge of God, and we take captive every thought to make it obedient to Christ."

Luke 14:27 (NLT) Jesus lets us know that a true disciple must first commit spiritually, carry their cross, to follow.

Proverbs 27:17 (NASB) "As iron sharpens iron, so one person sharpens another."

Prayer

Thank You, Yahweh, Father I am filled with wonder of You. Here I surrender myself to You, Alpha and Omega, the beginning, and the end. You have begun a work in me, and You are faithful to complete it. You have come to live in me. Direct me, shape me, and prepare me for the opportunities that You put before me. Give me the understanding to respond appropriately to every opportunity the small and future great ones. I don't want to miss anything You have for me. Open my eyes wide so I can see as You do to discern the time and move in the direction as ordained by You. Amen.

How do know an opportunity is indeed an opportunity? I am leaning into the direction of His Spirit in all things

KEY FIVE

Know Your Enemy

As a citizen of heaven and a visitor on this Earth you have to learn the tactics of the enemy to resist him. For years in my prayers, I have been vigilant what The Word has said to me about the enemy. Sometimes it seems we may have to repeat these words as reminders so as to not get fooled by him. My favorite all-time scripture is in *John 10:10 (NASB), "The thief comes only in order to steal and kill and destroy. I came that they may have and enjoy life, and have it in abundance [to the full, till it overflows]."* Note the only reason or intent of the enemy is to steal, kill and destroy. Keep alert for according to *First Peter 5:8 (AMP), "Be sober, be alert and cautious at all times. That enemy of yours, the devil, prowls around like a roaring lion [fiercely hungry], seeking someone to devour."* These scriptures or words are close to me. The enemy, devil, Satan - is the father of lies. *John 8:44 (AMP)* tells us, *"He was a murderer from the beginning and was against the truth, because there is no truth in him. When he tells a lie, he shows what he is really like, because he is a liar and the father of lies."* The enemy is real, alive, and active. Ignoring the enemy is equal to believing he will just go away if I don't resist him or pray against him, he will do me no harm. All of these misconceptions and deceptions are the very traps the enemy will plant, make you believe, and then you are subject to his tactics. He is a deceiver.

Years ago, I had the opportunity to write and teach a leadership curriculum to 12th grade students at a high school. One of my required readings was the timeless classic *The Art of War* by Sun Tzu. *The Art of War* offers insightful tactics to practice when we encounter an enemy. The tactics that I taught years ago still remain with me. The Bible provides the same tactics to engage and defeat the enemy. Let's look at these lessons of truth and direction to defeat the enemy every time.

In military tactics anyone engaged in war comes through the authority of a king, ruler, government, or nation. The power of the warrior is through whatever strength, force, or ability they are using to engage in the war. As a believer our authority is in the name of Jesus. In *Matthew 10:1 (NKJV)* we can see, "*… He gave them power over unclean spirits, to cast them out, and to heal all kinds of sickness and all kinds of disease."* Our power is in The Holy Spirit. The enemy recognizes power and authority and anyone who can exercise their power and authority will consistently defeat the enemy. So, our first tactic in defeating the enemy is knowing who you are or whose you are over the enemy. The enemy is a created being, a fallen angel that was never given any authority before the fall or after over you, a child of God. You have been created in the image of God with the inherited abilities as His child. *"Behold, I give you the authority to trample on serpents and scorpions, and over all the power of the enemy, and nothing shall by any means hurt you,"* (Luke 10:19, NKJV).

Our second tactic lies in our creation. You are a spirit that lives in a human body with a soul. You are able to do all the things Jesus the Son demonstrated in His time on this Earth. Now take a hold of that for a moment before you move quickly past this. Sun Tzu says, "If you know the enemy and know yourself, you need not fear the result of a hundred battles. If you know yourself but not the enemy, for every victory gained you will also suffer a defeat. If you know neither the enemy nor yourself, you will succumb in every battle." To be in the war with an enemy and never know your power or authority has already set you up for defeat. The battle has been fought and won, even before you engage in the war.

Another sure tactic in knowing your enemy is knowing the power in which they operate. Sun Tzu says, "So in war, the way is to avoid what is strong, and strike at what is weak." Your power, your strength is in The Holy Spirit. "... *His power toward us who believe, according to the working of His mighty power." (Ephesians 1:19, NKJV).* You can't effectively engage in the war without The Word. In *Hebrews 4:12 (NKJV) we* know that "... *the word of God is living and powerful, and sharper than any two-edged sword, piercing even to the division of soul and spirit, and of joints and marrow, and is a discerner of the thoughts and intents of the heart."* You need to know what you have, and The Word provides that knowledge, but knowledge is not enough without the revelation of The Holy Spirit.

Prayer and The Word is your source of power without it you are vulnerable to the strikes of the enemy. I cannot say the enemy has you pegged if you are not in connection to your power source, but I can surely attest that he will use the same tactics he used on Jesus, your Father. Remember in the wilderness he twisted The Word and tried to get Jesus to prove His power. He even attempted to get Jesus to bow down to him. Every encounter Jesus combated the enemy He used The Word and His authority. The enemy is always looking to oppress you with his power and to gain control over you. If you are not sure of your relationship and position in Christ as a believer, he will have you begging for mercy subjugated fearfully to his authority.

The enemy is known as the father of lies. *John 8:44 (NKJV), "...there is no truth in him...he is a liar and the father of it."* Some say in every lie there is a truth, twisted truth. The problem is that partial truth is a lie and recognizing the underlying truth may in fact fool you into believing it is not a lie. Now liars are close relatives of cheaters, thieves, gossipers, and any chaotic division. Think about it. What is the purpose of a lie but to hide the truth, sabotage a truth, sending everything into a tailspin of confusion? I do not want to say this is the only problem you will encounter, but I can sure attest to you that this tactic of the enemy is so thoroughly comprehensive that it is enough to wipe you out and send you flailing for help. How do you deal with lies? Stand on the truth. Part of your weapon of warfare is the sword of the spirit, The Word of God. Take notice a sword is active, engaged in the battle; it is an active part of the soldiers' equipment defending and fending off the enemy at every turn or opposition. The sword is always engaged in the battle.

As a believer you must believe and know you can never compromise with the enemy; do not relinquish your power and authority. You, as a child of God, made in His image has everything you need to stand against the enemy, and like most things the more you are aware and prepared the better you will be in learning his tactics. Sun Tzu says, "Rouse him, and learn the principle of his activity or inactivity. Force him to reveal himself, to find out his vulnerable spots." You have the upper hand, the advantage, and the judge in your court. Do not allow the enemy to walk away a victor in this battle when defeat is his position.

> *Hebrews 4:12 (NKJV) "The Word of God is living and powerful, and sharper than any two-edged sword, piercing even to the division of soul and spirit."*
>
> *Matthew 10:1 (NKJV) "He gave them power over unclean spirits, to cast them*

out, and to heal all kinds of sickness and all kinds of disease."

Ephesians 6:17 (NKJV) "And take the helmet of salvation, and the sword of the spirit, which is the word of God..."

Prayer

Father in Your mighty name I can encounter the battles with the enemy and win. Every struggle that I encounter has already been won. Thank you for always being there and winning every one of my battles. Your hand never grows weary; Your promise never fails even when I do not know the path that I should take. You never leave me, even though many run and scatter, You are there in every struggle. I cast out the works of darkness and expose their lies. In You I have peace and assurance that I am a victor in every area of my life.
Amen.

How do I know how to defeat the enemy? I stand on The Word of truth in every battle; God always wins.

Confront Your Enemy

Knowing the tactics of the enemy is pointless if we are not willing to have an out and out confrontation with him. I know we all would prefer to be left alone especially if we are talking about the enemy, but the truth is the enemy will not cease to bother you because you are not willing to take up his challenge. *Ephesians 6:10-11 (NASB)* reminds us to *"… be strong in the Lord and in the strength of His might. Put on the full armor of God, so that you will be able to stand firm against the schemes of the devil."* As you hide for cover you become the victim and not the victor that God designed you to be. The enemy will never cease as long as you are a child of God and if he does, you may want to check to see if your relationship with God is still on fire. How do we go about engaging with the enemy, confronting him and his wiles, and putting him under your feet? We don't fight with flesh and blood but against principalities and powers of darkness. We engage with the enemy on the spiritual level by taking up the armor of God and engaging every piece of the spiritual weapons: truth from The Word, righteousness, The Gospel of peace, faith, salvation, and the sword of the spirit.

Do we pick the fight or wait for the encounter? Have you ever had a bully in your life or worse an annoying friend that you just can't lose? Well, that is how the enemy will show up; an obvious foe trying to subjugate you or a seeming friend that looks to destroy you. Either way he is still an enemy, not a person or situation, but a spiritual principality to be fought with spiritual tools.

My encounters with the enemy always take me back to Jesus. What would Jesus do? Now it may seem corny, but it is true and that is my absolute best example to follow or even share with you. When the enemy encounters Jesus and He is accused, questioned by Herod, He answered him nothing. He doesn't defend himself. Instead, we find in *Luke 23:9-10 (NKJV), "Then he questioned Him with many words, but He answered him nothing. And the chief priests and scribes stood and vehemently accused Him."* When accused by our enemy, we naturally look to defend ourselves. By profession I teach, instruct, provide guidance, and direction. Sometimes because of the nature of my profession I may be the only one really talking while trying to get students engaged in the conversation and discussion. I have a lot to say but I have realized through the leading of the spirit my words carry power and so does the silence in my voice. There is power in not speaking because my very silence can overpower the enemy. When I say nothing, I surrender myself to the power of The Spirit and the spirit realm comes into full operation because I am surrendering to God. God intercedes on my behalf. I have wondered when Jesus was getting accused what was He thinking about. Was He praying for God's intercession, anticipating an opportunity to speak or was He just submitting to the power of The Spirit to transform and move the situation forward? In my silence I have prayed every word that the Lord has given me for the situation. I have decreed the blessings the Lord has promised me according to His Word and I have cursed the enemy and his tactics against me. I have called out all the promises of God for my very situation. The more I have relied on the spirit the more I see how His transformation is complete and comprehensive in the situation. Silence and submission are not weaknesses, but when I am less God is more powerful, interceding for me. When I am weak, He is strong.

Then there are times that God gives a direction, a word that stays with me forever. You don't forget that word for years it will remind you of The Word that God gave, and it will encourage you to trust every word God speaks to you. Over a lifetime of listening, you can have many words but listening and doing go hand in hand. What I mean by this is when God gives you word it is the direction to take, the way you should go. I can remember a word when I was twelve as gunshots rang out around me and my cousins scrambled for safety. The direction God gave was simple and direct, "Go behind the cans in the alley." There really wasn't any time for me to think or wonder was there any place better. I trusted The Word God was giving me and I ran to the shelter unaware of where my cousins had hidden or if the gunman was coming back around for another aim at us. You have to know that The Word God will give you is like no other. I am talking about absolute confidence in Him. That word from God saved my life from a racist trying to kill some kids walking in their own neighborhood. Another time The Word came, "Answer the call" that call changed my life. Please know that every word God will give you is important; there is no insignificant word. Each word is life even if it makes no sense. A word can be quiet in your spirit or for me many times it will be in a dream or vision. I want to hear all of them so all of them I want to respond appropriately. If you ask God for an answer expect an answer, so don't be surprised when you get The Word. Your job is to respond.

> *Ephesians 6:10-11 (NKJV) "...be strong in the Lord and in the strength of His might."*

> *Psalm 144:1 (NKJV) "Blessed be the Lord my Rock, Who trains my hands for war, And my fingers for battle—"*

> *Proverbs 3:5-6 (NKJV) "Trust in the Lord with all your heart and lean not on your own understanding; In all your ways acknowledge Him, And He shall direct your paths."*

> *Hebrews 6:12 (NKJV) "...that you do not become [a]sluggish but imitate those who through faith and patience inherit the promises."*

Prayer

Lord, You train me to wage war with my enemy. Thank You for Your Word that gives me wisdom and teaches me to wage war with my enemy. Your words direct my paths. All victory belongs to You. I pray for Your strategies. Show me the way I should go this day. I believe in Your Word that gives me all power. Welcome Holy Spirit into my situation to teach me all things. I am praying for Your will to direct my prayers Amen.

How do I face my enemy? I stand on the power of God to face the enemy. When I am weak, He is strong.

Loving The Unlovable

What makes me so different from the rest of the world? Why would someone seek you out from the rest of the crowd? Simply what will make you so exceptional in your everyday tasks, neighborhood, or job? Love is the distinguishing feature of Christ-followers. The only debt I owe humanity is love. Love is who we are daily. Love speaks volumes in every situation, to the needy, and even ourselves. The lack of love in a person's life is not easily recognized. We do not think, oh, he is so rude because he feels unloved. Or why is she so mean to me when she is jealous of the love, I demonstrate despite her? Love is a cure-all, and I am not trying to be a cliché. It does work, but we must first get past ourselves, our sense of being right, affirmed by the very people who are our source of pain. From the years working with people and teaching students across the spectrum, I have realized that love has been the single factor that changes everything.

How do I love the unlovable? Can I show my love for those refusing to be loved? Do I love a stranger? Where do I start? Years ago, I learned that to discipline a student; I first must have a relationship with them to speak into their lives. Anything outside of disciplining without connection will breed resentment, anger, rebellion, or shutdown. How we respond demonstrates our love. You can mistreat me, lie, or even curse me, but my response will consistently show the love God has for me by sending His Son to die for us on the cross. What looks like God's love?

Sometimes, my love for the enemy has been praying for their needs, problems, desires, and health. Now they will not know you prayed for them unless you decide to tell, which I do not suggest unless it is for God's glory and not yours. Your prayer will change you too. I have had supervisors that looked like they hated me, but The Word God gave me was to pray for them. Not just pray for my good and protection but their needs that were seen and unseen. My enemies never come off my prayer list. Sometimes in my prayers, God has revealed that no one has ever prayed for them. Some people are not fortunate enough to have been born into a Christian praying family and what you see is the result of that lack in their life. I can disregard their injustice and still keep to the purpose of my role or position in their lives.

I never concede to their injustice or rudeness, but I kill them with kindness. Love in their eyes is undeserved; we overlook those actions to achieve the greater purpose in their lives and your own. In the scripture in *Romans 12:20-21 (NKJV)*, the Lord says, *"If your enemy is hungry, feed him; If he is thirsty, give him a drink; For in so doing you will heap coals of fire on his head."* Do not be overcome by evil but overcome evil with good. From my experiences, I have seen some astounding results from this action, and that has been far more rewarding than me digging my heels in and hating them even more. I may never see His vengeance or the result of them planting bad seed or wickedness in my life, but I will trust God's justice. God can do more than you could ever in dealing with the unloved in your whole lifetime. I say, Lord, have your way even in this. God has never failed me in this, and I have been able to see the sudden happenings of God. What seems abrupt to us is God's work, justice in motion. In *Deuteronomy 7:3-5 (NKJV), "For they will turn your sons away from following Me, to serve other gods; so, the anger of the Lord will be aroused against you and destroy you suddenly."* God does not contradict His character, but His justice will always prevail yesterday, today, and tomorrow.

This love for my enemy can change lives. Every year my students try desperately to figure out my favorite class or the favorite student. I giggle at their guesses because the most unlovable class or students always will profess first that they are my favorite. In hearing this, I know loving them does work. I usually smile, and they go away very content that my teacher loves me the most, and I love her too. Remember where I started? How can you discipline a student or speak into someone's life? Love people first; then you can extend a relationship with them which will allow you to impart God's Word into their lives.

> *First Corinthians 13:1-2 (NKJV) "Though I speak with the tongues of men and angels but have not love, I have become sounding brass or a clanging cymbal. And though I bestow all my goods to feed the poor, and though I give my body to be burned, but have not love, it profits me nothing."*

Matthew 5:43-48 (NKJV) 'You shall love your neighbor and hate your enemy.' But I say to you, love your enemies, bless those who curse you, do good to those who hate you, and pray for those who spitefully use you and persecute you, that you may be sons of your Father in heaven; for He makes His sun rise on the evil and the good, and sends rain on the just and the unjust."

Prayer

God, You are love, and You love me. No one has ever loved me like You have all my life. You command me to love my neighbor, and my neighbor is the world. Teach me Your love for those that do not love me. Give me the supernatural ability to represent You in flesh form to love them. I know that You are transforming my love in unique ways to draw the unloved to You. My most significant opportunity to reach the lost is the love I demonstrate to them despite what they have done to me. Thank you, Father, for interceding and teaching me how to love in word and deed. Amen.

How do I win over my enemy? I love him like he has never been loved.

Words, Curses, and Threats

As a word scholar, I value the importance of well-chosen words to convey a message, to express a blessing, or even a curse. My expressions speak for me, and they can speak into my life to create my future. In *Ephesians 4:29 (NASB),* Paul tells us "*...not to let corrupting talk come out of our mouths, but only such as is suitable for building up, as fits the occasion, that it may give grace to those who hear.*"

I have always been a lover of words and vocabulary, amazed, enraptured by the beauty of words and their innumerable capabilities in conveying a message. As far back as I can remember, I have studied words, written words, played with their arrangement, and recognized the power of words. For me, The Bible is a masterful wordsmith conveying more than the written scriptures. I love mulling over the words and relishing the eloquent phrasing of scripture in the text. Unfortunately, growing up, the words I spoke created all kinds of problems for me. My words signaled offense, disrespect, damage, brutal honesty, and hurt. Over time I grew tired of saying I am sorry; the words were meaningless, and I vowed to be a watcher of my own words and guard the gate of my mouth. I would never have to say sorry ever again. Today my words are diplomatic, truthful, but tactful, and direct. They are honeyed up with a sauciness that makes the words palatable, weighed out, and sometimes thrown out for a better, more appropriate time. I accept my responsibility to convey a message that cares for the message and the receiver to achieve the purpose. I can say sorry because I am responsible for creating bridges, not burning them if I want my message heard.

I have also learned that words can live beyond our time. *Colossians 4:6 (NKJV)* admonishes us to, "*Let your speech always be gracious, seasoned with salt, so that you may know how you ought to answer each person."* Words plant and grow either weeds or flowers, but they never die. *Proverbs 16:24 (NKJV)* reminds us that, *"Pleasant words are like a honeycomb, Sweetness to the soul and health to the bone."* I can still remember some words people have spoken to me, and I am sure you could too if you wanted. Those words still live, so we are responsible for the words we speak. Early in my career, I recognized that my words had a life, and I did not want them to be running helter-skelter through someone's life with damaging effects. *Matthew 15:18-20 (NASB), "But what comes out of the mouth proceeds from the heart, and this defiles a person. Out of the heart come evil thoughts, murder, adultery, sexual immorality, theft, false witness, slander. These are what defile a person. But to eat with unwashed hands does not defile anyone."* Daily I prayed, "Let the words of my mouth and the meditations of my heart be acceptable in your sight, oh Lord," *(Psalm 19:14 NKJV).* I did not miss a day. Daily I had the opportunity to apply this scripture to my work with students, colleagues, and parents. I never want my words to create irreparable damage. Paul reminds us in *Romans 3:14-17 (NKJV)* what we are capable of in sin under the law, *"Their mouth is full of curses and bitterness. Their feet are swift to shed blood; in their paths are ruin and misery, and the way of peace they have not known."* I want my words to speak grace and hope to the hearers, even if for the first time in their lives.

Words are not just about the words we say to others but also about ourselves, our lives. The words we plant in our own lives curse our lives and threaten our future. *James 3:8-10 (NIV)* advises, *"But no human being can tame the tongue. It is a restless evil, full of deadly poison. We bless our Lord and Father, and with it, we curse people in the likeness of God. From the same mouth come blessing and cursing."* Those words, our words to ourselves, about ourselves, are just as important in our lives. *Colossians 3:8 (NASB), "But now you must put them all away: anger, wrath, malice, slander, and obscene talk from your mouth."* It is important to remember that our words affect the hearer, and the hearer can be you. For every negative comment a person will make, they will need to make five positive comments. Can you imagine the number we genuinely need to cancel the negative we have spoken in our own lives? Our words have put curses on our own lives. For example, we might say I will fail this test; I cannot do anything right; no one loves me; I am ugly, or no one cares about me. Every one of these statements will need at least five positive comments like my Father loves me. God cares for me. I can do all things in Christ. These negative comments, or curses block the blessings the Lord has for us in our lives. The enemy will plant negative words by even well-meaning people. These curses block our blessings and lead us to think we are not worthy of a blessing. So, our words and the words of others can threaten our tomorrow. Use your words wisely, speak The Word over your life, and others. Plant good seeds, so you can reap a harvest in due season.

What about those threats? What are you to do? How are you to respond? In my lifetime, I have had a few words of threats always from someone I know, not from random strangers, so the threats become personal. My response was never to respond. I always recognized the threat – again - because I am a communicator, not antagonizing or provoking them. I prayed God's direction and claimed the promise not to be troubled, but I did not do anything nothing but pray The Word promise God has given me for those times. *First Peter 3:14 (NKJV)* encourages us when it says, *"But even if you should suffer for righteousness' sake, you are blessed. And do not be afraid of their threats, nor be troubled."* Every word tells me not to be troubled or afraid, which is the message I communicate to my threats. *Isaiah 8:12 (NKJV)* speaks wisely in saying, *"Do not say, 'A conspiracy,' Concerning all that these people call a conspiracy, Nor be afraid of their threats, nor be troubled."* Threats are insults, promises to inflict pain, punishment to make a person comply, but the Lord tells us not even to be troubled by them. Threats are lies, twisted words to instill fear, provoke even anger, but each threat is again another attempt by the enemy to defeat The Word of God, plant a seed to dominate you, and kill the purpose God has called you. My threats have fizzled in their start, and I face them with The Word of God. Remember, weapons will form, but they will not prosper over you.

> *Proverbs 18:21 (NKJV) "Death and life are in the power of the tongue, And those who love it will eat its fruit."*

> *Colossians 3:8 (NKJV) "But now you yourselves are to put off all these: anger, wrath, malice, blasphemy, filthy language out of your mouth."*

> *Psalm 19:14 (NKJV) "Let the words of my mouth and the meditation of my heart Be acceptable in Your sight, O Lord, my strength and my Redeemer."*

> *First Peter 3:14 (NKJV) "But even if you should suffer for righteousness' sake, you are blessed. And do not be afraid of their threats, nor be troubled."*

Prayer

Lord, Your words give me life. Thank You for always giving me words that give new life in every area of my life. I confess that I have not always been wise in my words, repeating negative comments to myself and my future. I submit my words to You, so they honor You. Teach me and guide me as I study my words to always administer to the hearer and represent You. Let my words provide life to all those that I may encounter today.
Amen.

How do I direct my words? I speak with grace with words that encourage and uplift the hearer.

KEY SIX

Discipline by The Word

The Word discipline carries many negative stereotypes. If you hear the term, it is reminiscent of something painful, restrictive, and difficult, but the truth of the matter is discipline is the reward of your action. In school, discipline can mean your subject area, the action, plan taken or required to ensure a definite change. In all these context's discipline is acting upon the person, outside forces demanding an inward transformation. True change happens from the inside that is then evident from the outside. This change known as self-discipline does not have to be imposed by artificial restraints or mandates but is a personal coach guiding and directing actions and decisions. Everything in this life comes about as the result of discipline or the lack of it: a diet, fitness, graduation, job success, and even failure.

Years ago, as a middle school teacher I learned that I had to master the art of discipline to be effective in my classroom and most importantly for my students. My classroom discipline focused on improving my students not for English class only but for life. Students who can learn discipline can achieve great success both on an academic and personal level. Discipline that leads to self-discipline starts first with a plan of action. For a teacher, the plan of action can be class rules; in my personal life the plan of action can be personal goals. Whatever you may call it a plan of action must be written down. Keep the plan simple; it will be easy to keep and less intimidating to accomplish.

My class rules are never long and lengthy, but always reinforced. Reinforcing the plan will make it intrinsic and natural. A friend I had years ago always said, "Never give a rule you were not meaning to reinforce." I have a hard-fast rule about turning schoolwork in on time. This rule is also a personal rule that I have. I say turn in assignments before they are due to ensure you can meet your deadline. So, I then must plan, provide class activities and assignments to ensure students are moving toward the due date and teach the necessary tools to ensure that students can meet the goal. I teach my students how to meet a deadline and the steps to take to get there. Learning self-discipline like any discipline can be a learned behavior, if necessary. Do they always get it right? No, but they know that I always make provisions for them to succeed and support them through the process. Reinforcing can come in many ways so keep that in mind, some seem negative, but pushing or supportive encouragement past the pain will reinforce the expectation.

Be consistent until it is methodical. Sometimes discipline can seem stifling, but I have to say it can be reassuring and comforting because it is predictable; it is fair. Consistency is the glue to self-discipline. If I consistently reinforce the code of conduct in my classroom, students are more likely to accept it, appreciate it, respect it, and the best I have seen reinforce it without me ever saying a word to other students or outsiders. In life, many things are not comforting to the soul, but a consistent rule of thumb to follow can provide sanity in your chaos. Will this always produce the results I want in my personal goals or classroom expectations? Maybe not, so then I must learn to pick up where I fail. How do I pick up students when they fail? One of the best methods I learned in classroom discipline from my middle school teacher years was that every day you get to start over. The marks or checks that failed a student yesterday do not exist today as a matter fact today I do not even remember them. So, knowing you can start again without the limitations of past failures helps you learn from your failure to embrace your future. This is liberating. I can liberate myself.

At times students who have failed my class or test will begin to make promises of a better tomorrow that they will not fail again. I listen but what I really want to try to get out of them is what they have learned and what do they need to do differently to not fail again. I reinforce the failure is not a failure if you have learned in the process about yourself or how to handle a situation better. I am trying to have them revise a plan of action that is considerate of them on a personal level. Self-discipline is a plan of action intrinsically and consistently reinforced to ensure success for my future.

Hebrews 12:11 (NKJV) "For the moment, all discipline seems not to be pleasant, but painful; yet to those who have been trained by it, afterward it yields the peaceful fruit of righteousness."

Proverbs 12:1 (NASB) "One who loves discipline loves knowledge, but one who hates rebuke is stupid."

Proverbs 15:32 (NASB) One who neglects discipline rejects himself, but one who listens to a rebuke acquires understanding.

> **Prayer**
>
> *Father, You always care for me. Even when my path has strayed You have never failed to guide me back to Your truth. Your love for me surrounds me. You have never left me even when I have walked my own way. Your discipline has been a guide in my life. It gives me the wisdom I need to grow and flourish in this life both physically and spiritually. Your knowledge is life for me. Your discipline gives me new life to understand what you have for me. I know that your discipline in my life will lead to my success. Amen.*

How can I become disciplined? I apply my heart to discipline and my ears to words of knowledge.

The Word

In all of history there is not one single book like The Bible, Scripture, Word of God. Nowhere. The Bible at one time was the only source of learning for generations. Principles and laws of our country originated from The Bible. It is still the founding source of truth, still practiced, and held sacred. The finest piece of literature that encompasses absolutely everything: histories, genealogies, wars, rejection, freedom, love, forgiveness, and hatred. The power behind The Word is transformative. The Word planted in the believer's heart creates a life changing transformation like nothing ever experienced outside of the salvation experience.

How can a sinner change his ways, transform into a Christ follower? It is The Word. Our mind is a depository, receiving and collecting ideas, concepts continuously to eliminate a thought, or to replace a thought an exchange happens, a deposit. The Word mindset comes to mind because to reset your mind there must be something, an impetus that triggers a change. *"And do not be conformed to this world, but be transformed by the renewing of your mind, that you may prove what is that good and acceptable and perfect will of God,"* (Romans 12:2, NKJV). Transformed, our minds need renewal, so we can be part of the work God has called us individually to.

The Word is our life source without it we do not have the power to resist our old way of thinking. The Word transforms and is food for our spirit man. Jesus said in *Matthew 4:4 (NKJV), "It is written, 'Man shall not live by bread alone, but by every word that proceeds from the mouth of God.'"* When I first became interested in reading The Word it was dry routine and frankly very confusing; it was an obligation, a duty. I wondered how someone could read The Bible and find any joy in reading it. Then I decided to read to know about Jesus, His great transformation on the Earth, and His ministry while He was here. I read as a new convert wanting to learn everything I could about God and how to live this life of a believer. The Word became a search for both knowledge and encouragement. I read a lot of The Gospel following Jesus around, listening in on His miracles, and watching His public appeal to sinners and I thought I would love to be Jesus' friend. He always knew His purpose and direction and frankly nothing deterred Him from His goal even when the goal was so unappealing.

I have read The Bible as a student, believer, intercessor, Bible study leader, disciple, parent, teacher, friend, wife, daughter, sinner, outcast, giver, divorcee, single, and it is never the same - even if I read the same passage. Getting a new mind does not just happen one time but it requires changing increasingly into the image of God. In *Second Corinthians 3:18 (AMP)* Paul writes, *"And we all, with unveiled face, continually seeing as in a mirror the glory of the Lord, are progressively being transformed into His image from [one degree of] glory to [even more] glory, which comes from the Lord, [who is] the spirit."* We must actively pursue The Word in our lives. As a teacher, The Word is a lifeline to all God has for me. I try to keep The Word on my tongue even when I am speaking to the students because it can transform lives. Memorizing The Word is extremely helpful and comforting. Years ago, when my mother was no longer able to see the written word on the pages because of poor eyesight she would quote The Word buried in her spirit. That experience helped me realize the power of knowing The Word. Sometimes, we cannot read the text or turn the page. Also, even if you are not a person with great memory ability simply by reading The Word, the spirit will help you remember what is needed at the appropriate time.

John 14:26 (NKJV) "But the Helper, The Holy Spirit, whom The Father will send in My name, He will teach you all things, and bring to your remembrance all things that I said to you."

Romans 12:2 (NKJV) "Be transformed by the renewing of your mind, that you may prove what is that good and acceptable and perfect will of God."

Second Corinthians 3:18 (NASB) "Being transformed into the same image from glory to glory, just as [a]by the spirit of the Lord."

Prayer

The Word is a light unto my path and in it there is life. Let The Word guide me into all truth. God's Word transforms my mind, so I transform in the image of Christ. I am a child of God and I need the transformation of Your Word to renew my mind and spirit. Lord let Your Word give me new ideas and strategies to move in the things You have designed for me. Amen.

How can I renew my mind? The Word of God transforms and teaches me all things.

1. Choose to think differently. We have the mind of Christ *(First Corinthians 2:16, NASB).* Thinking differently is an active decision. Make a choice. We become what we believe.

2. Read The Word daily to fill your mind with God's truth. You have to replace your thinking with good thinking. The Word and The Holy Spirit working together transforms your thinking. *Second Timothy 3:16 (NLT) "All Scripture is inspired by God and is useful to teach us what is true and to make us realize what is wrong in our lives."*

3. Hold every thought captive. The Word reminds us in *Second Corinthians 10:5 (NASB) "We are destroying arguments and all arrogance raised against the knowledge of God, and we are taking every thought captive to the obedience of Christ..."*

4. Replace your thoughts with The Word. As you are more conscious of your thoughts, replace your negative thoughts with God's thoughts. Transform your mind by practicing the thoughts

of God, i.e., love, peace, joy this will change the structure of your thinking daily. When you recognize a thinking pattern that is destructive pray to God to renew your mind in that area. Study The Word for those areas and apply those words to your mindset that is destructive for you.

Renewing your mind is a daily practice. According to recent brain research, conducted by psychology experts at Queen's University in Canada, the average person has 6000 thoughts per day. Every day we have to hold our thoughts and redirect them before they destroy our thinking and beliefs.

Praying for Wisdom

The wisdom of the Lord nourishes the soul. Wisdom comes from above and unless I am talking and communing with God, I do not have that wisdom. The two, wisdom and knowledge, are different. Knowledge is acquired by reading, The Bible included, but the application of that knowledge at the appropriate or perfect time is wisdom acquired from an all-knowing God. It is common knowledge that everything you learn in teacher college is theory, knowledge. The knowledge actually in many ways is just information. Ask any teacher, the true test of wisdom in school happens in the classroom and not in the textbook. For example, in teacher school you will learn about lesson planning, in fact planning lessons and developing the curriculum is prime but, in the classroom, you quickly learn the curriculum becomes secondary to the student connection. Students don't care about the curriculum, and you will be remiss if the curriculum is the center of your classroom instruction. In the same way I can read The Word and, yes, there is wisdom there; but the most profound intimate wisdom that God imparts is through my relationship with Him. This is the same in the classroom. I can know the curriculum, but the wisdom that I need to get that curriculum across to the student happens in my relationship with the student. Students want to know you see and know them before they care enough to truly learn any curriculum set before them. God gives me the understanding I need to apply the wisdom that The Word imparts *(First Corinthians 2:6 -16)*.

Wisdom sounds lofty, even deep and it is. Wisdom comes from God, and we know that God is all powerful, deep, and lofty. What is the difference between wisdom of the world and God? Worldly wisdom has all the sinful characteristics of the world. Worldly wisdom is self-serving, unforgiving, intimidating, revengeful, unmerciful, harsh, pushy, and partial. Look at some of the famous worldly wisdom adages: If you want to go fast go alone. The early bird gets the worm. Keep your friends close and your enemies closer. Godly wisdom is above all other wisdom in your life. Some provide warnings such as, *"Behold, I am sending you out as sheep in the midst of wolves; so be as wary as serpents, and as innocent as doves,"* (Matthew 10:16, NASB). Other words provide success in life like, *Proverbs 13:20 (NLT), "Walk with the wise and become wise, for a companion of fools suffers harm." Proverbs 15:12, in the same translation,* tells me, *"Mockers resent correction, so they avoid the wise."* The wisdom of God is pure, not forceful, or bias. It is a gentle guide directing your path without partiality. James tells us that Godly wisdom *"...wiling to yield, full of mercy and good fruits ... without hypocrisy,"* (James 3:17, NASB). You cannot find any wisdom compared to the wisdom of God. *"Wisdom is the principal thing; therefore, get understanding,"* (Proverbs 4:7, NASB).

In the varying decisions facing us, we need a source that is reliable and trustworthy. As I search for the path to take in a situation it is the wisdom of God that I listen for before making my next steps, because nothing can compare to the wisdom that God can provide. Godly wisdom always promises a resolution that is all encompassing, gentle, and merciful. God is who I want to hear from, and I want people to see God in me, my choices, and my decisions.

The wisdom writer of the Biblical book of Proverbs, King Solomon, gives both wisdom and instruction. Practical wisdom so you may live your life. As a single mother, with all my family in different parts of the country, I only had God. My mom and maternal family have long gone onto glory, and I never had an extended group of friends. Growing up my girls did not have the confusion of mixed messages about living life. When I was raising my daughters, I read Proverbs repeatedly for every situation. Proverbs provides an answer for everything. I did not want to be the parent that said I said so; I wanted to plant The Word in their heart because it would never come back void. My girls can still quote those scriptures that guided their everyday lives. In chapter one of Proverbs, the writer tells us that wisdom goes hand in hand with instruction, and application of the wisdom. When you receive wisdom examine it and understand what has been said, then direct your decisions to move forward.

God freely gives wisdom, and we need to ask for wisdom to instruct us in our living. In times past, when I sought a word from God, it came as a quiet answer placed in my soul. Sometimes that answer seemed so obvious and simple, gentle. If we lack wisdom, ask of God *"... who gives to all liberally and without reproach..." (James 1:5, NASB).* The beauty of God's wisdom, as expressed in Proverbs, is that it covers a wide array of answers, and can be exactly the answer needed at the same time. The wisdom of God has no limit and can provide answers for ages to come. The Bible tells us there is nothing new under the sun and we can see that a book written in

686 BC is still relevant in its instructing and providing knowledge. God's wisdom will uncover situations and provide the wisdom you need to navigate through them. He has declared to His people the power of His works (*Psalm 110:6*). Wisdom gives might, strength, and authority. Wisdom will give you the ability to persevere.

> *James 1:5 (NASB) "if we lack wisdom ask of God "...who gives to all liberally and without reproach..."*

> *James 3:17 (NASB) Godly wisdom "...wiling to yield, full of mercy and good fruits ... without hypocrisy."*

> *Proverbs 4:6 (NASB) "Do not forsake her, and she will preserve you; Love her, and she will keep you."*

> *Proverbs 4:7 (NASB) "Wisdom is the principal thing; therefore, get wisdom."*

Prayer:

Righteous Father You are all-knowing, and Your Word is everlasting through all times. I pray this day for Your supernatural wisdom over my circumstances and my mental and physical being. May Your wisdom reign over all that concerns me. I give You my ears and heart to speak to me in my life daily. Teach me how to war with Godly wisdom to defeat my enemy on every level. May You have the glory over my life teach me Your ways.
Amen.

How do I walk in God's wisdom? I read The Bible to learn the wisdom of God and practice by applying it daily to my life circumstances.

Work as Unto the Lord

Work, the dreaded word that crosses every person's lips at some point in their life. Do we sometimes think we have a greater purpose than this job, this employer, or an assigned task? Everyone has an opinion about work. Some thoughts are negative, some positive, but it all depends on the why of your work. When I was growing up, work was for adults. Anytime I mentioned the idea, it was something put off on others or adults, something you had to do later when you grow up. Work was a rite of passage. My father would say you have the rest of your life to work, so concentrate on your schoolwork. At sixteen, when I got a job at a local place, my dad forced me to quit it after only one day on the job. Again, the message conveyed "you have the rest of your life to work." My father also believed that work was necessary for living, and it did not matter the type of work you had to do to get paid. He felt no work was ever too demeaning to do. One of the most lasting work speeches I remember growing up from my father was if someone has a need, a job that you can do, do it and accept payment, no handouts. If they need the job and you can do it even if it seems easy to you or obvious, they are still requesting a service that you should receive compensation. I grew up seeing work ethics in my immediate and distant family households, from my home to a distant aunt. Everyone took work very seriously, and work was not just a paycheck or reduced to a number but as a service, a gift that can contribute to the world and provide a service to those who needed the work.

The revelation that my work is a Godly service came later as I joined the workforce as an adult. Yes, work is our calling. God created the Earth and placed man and then woman in the garden. They had all they needed. Work was given from the beginning to man, *"The Lord God placed the man in the Garden of Eden to tend and watch over it," (Genesis 2:18, NLT).* In the middle of Eden, the garden, was the tree of the knowledge of good and evil. The Lord had told the man and woman not to eat from this tree, but in their disobedience, they listened to the shrewdest animal, the serpent. The woman was tempted by the serpent to eat from the tree and then she gave some to her husband. Once they had eaten from the tree their eyes were opened, and they felt shame at their nakedness. God placed curses on the man, woman, and the serpent *(Genesis 3:13-19, NLT).* The man was cursed since he listened to his wife and ate of the tree. *"...the ground is cursed because of you. All of your life you will struggle to scratch a living from it," (Genesis 3:17, NLT).* After the fall, a curse was placed on man indicating that he would spend his time on Earth working. *Colossians 3:23 (NKJV)* tells us, *"And whatever you do, do it heartily, as to the Lord and not to men."* How do you keep the focus, work pass the pain, disregarded, or overlooked at work? It is easy to say you are not working for your employer, but God, which is easier said than done. My first thought on Monday morning when the alarm sounds at 5:15 is not again and pain - not that I am serving God. We need more teeth to move forward in working for God. Our work is the reasonable service that we get to share in the work that God has given each of us individually to contribute to this Earth. When I think that my work can change a life or minister to someone, I am honored to provide the service. And to know that my service transcends this Earth is excellent, and The Father in heaven has allowed you and me to partake in the greater mission to this Earth.

Just like you, somedays I am not enthusiastic or honored, but frustrated and even disappointed. But to keep the momentum, we need a more significant purpose, a bigger picture in this life to move forward, a vision. In *Habakkuk 2:2 (NIV), "Then the Lord answered me and said: 'Write the vision And make it plain on tablets, That he may run who reads it.'"* Small thinking, even self-thinking, will keep us frozen in the present, stuck in the here and now. God has an extensive view of our contribution to the work that we do daily. Everyone's work is necessary for our society, and every person encounters different people to communicate and contribute to God's purpose for their work. God's work perspective is so ingenious little old you and me can have a part in the vision. I, like you, sometimes feel discouraged, unappreciated, and defeated, but I examine why I feel this way in those times. Did I get in the way of myself? Did I want the glory or recognition when in truth, God is the gift giver, and He owns even the gift? Like other things, the Lord allows me to use my talent to make a living and serve my community.

My gift is worship; we get to invest in that gift, and our faithfulness, commitment to this gift opens new opportunities for our gifts to grow and different areas open to us. My work honors God just like my money. A tithe is a form of worship; all of it is my worship, and I get the opportunity to nurture that gift. Do you ever wonder why some people supersede others in opportunities or gifts? Are they more blessed or gifted? We are charged with the task of managing the gift by the gift giver, God. In *Matthew 25:14-28,* we are introduced to the parables or stories, Jesus used to teach His disciples about The Kingdom of Heaven. One of the parables is of the three servants. The master is going away on a long journey, and he wanted to entrust his servants with his money, talents. He gives talents to each servant. One servant hid his talent and preserved it for safekeeping, another invested the gift, and it grew into more, and the last went to work and earned two more. The master reprimanded the servant who held onto his talent for safekeeping. You might be thinking at least he did not lose it. The truth is we do not lose our abilities or gifts given to us, but how we use them can provide us with more, and that is a good and acceptable offering to the Lord in our worship of Him. Work is our opportunity our test how we are responsible with our gifts.

I am a doer. I am practical, and my most significant concern is maximizing my gifts and being accountable for my talents, service, and worship to God. I look for opportunities to build and nurture my blessings, and I know God uses every experience. I must worship Him to learn how to use the skill. To keep your work, you must go for the long haul see into the future for the most incredible mission God has given to humanity. We serve and minister in every area of this Earth all over the planet. We get to be participators in the vision.

> *Habakkuk 2:2 (NIV) "Then the Lord answered me and said: "Write the vision And make it plain on tablets, That he may run who reads it."*

> *Proverbs 16:33 (NLT) "We may throw the dice, but the Lord determines how they fall."*

> *Colossians 3:23 (NLT) "Work willingly at whatever you do, as though you were working for the Lord rather than for people."*

> ## Prayer
>
> *Lord, Father, I know You are the giver of all my gifts and talents. Thank You for trusting me with the skills that You have given me. I embrace the path that You have given me to invest in my gift. Please show me Your way with this gift, direct my paths to honor and worship You. Give me Your vision, not my tunnel vision with my given skills. Give me a Godly perspective as you lead me, strategies to optimize my talents, and clarity for my life. Let my talents reach all those You have called to me.*
> *Amen.*

How do I do my work? I work knowing my work transcends Heaven and Earth. My Father will take care of the rest.

KEY SEVEN

Relationships, The Ambassadors

When we think about relationships, our first thought might wander to a marriage bond, or we look at boyfriend and girlfriend relations. Marriage, girlfriends, boyfriends, and parent relationships all begin with our first bond - Christ. The Lord communicated to me several years ago, "I did not create couples; I created individuals; I created you with you in mind." When God fashioned you and me, He never formed us with our spouse in mind. Each of us has an individual purpose, destiny and it is ours to fulfill regardless of the relationship. Yes, your parents or significant other can positively and negatively affect your future, but they do not determine the purpose that God has given you.

First, we are in connection with our Lord, and then we are in association with others. What do we mean by relationship? In the dictionary, relationship means connection, association, or kinship, an emotional connection, or sexual involvement. Our rapport with Christ predicates our association with others. If we can relate with people every day and not see them, then our connection suffers.

If we have a growing affiliation with God and ignore His heart, our relationship with others suffers. The relationship that we have with God will impact our relationship with others. Examine how you are in a relationship with God, then reflect on your relationship with people. Is it the same? Is it vastly different? Now, consider your responses. It is tough to allow people into spaces that have not included God.

Now I realize my growing relationship with God has evolved, and over time, in my relationship with Christ, I have grown more intimate, more in tune, and coordinated with The Father. But if we are not open to God in a relationship, knowing He is good to us and loves us, knows everything about us, then I will not be naturally open to a relationship with others. My relationship with others benefits from the relationship I have with The Father. *Luke 10:27 (NLT)* tells me, *"'Love the Lord your God with all your heart, soul, strength and with all your mind;' and 'Love your neighbor as yourself."* Because God loves me unconditionally, I also should look to love as He does. I know God recognizes everything about me, but I never suffer for that knowledge in any way. God loves me as an individual, knowing that love sends a message of value and worth. God loves me like that, and He knows all of me.

The beauty of teaching allows you to see the world right there in your classroom. Even though I am a teacher of English, I have also been a teacher of English to speakers of other languages. I can visit Israel, Haiti, Venezuela, France, Poland, Russia, Columbia, Mexico, Puerto Rico, Cuba, Africa, and even Egypt in one place. Every child I encounter comes to that classroom with value and worth, individual talents, and proclivities. Even though I only have ten months with these students, I love them just where I meet them. I do not know their past or future, but I know that the relationship I can foster with them over those months can reinforce their value and worth and be a source of change, growth, and transformation.

Our relationships with others are important in all of our lives. In education it is always part of a teacher evaluation; knowledge of learners, communication and learning environment are three standards involving relationships in my evaluation. Every profession in some way entails relationships. We were created as social beings. In Bible the Book of Ephesians in chapter 5 provides a list of relationships and our position in those relationships. In *Ephesians 5:21 (NKJV)* we find, *"Speak filled with the spirit, in psalms and spiritual songs, and make melody in your heart to the Lord. Give thanks for all things to God The Father. We are submitting to one another in fear of God."* The passage tells me that our relationship with others should be Spirit lead, not flesh lead, *"be filled with the spirit."* Spirit-led relationship looks like us speaking psalms, hymns, and The Word into each other's lives, making joy in our heart to the Lord, thanking God for all things, and most importantly, submitting one to another in fear of God. When our relationships are Spirit-led, the self cannot get in the way and has no place, then we can freely submit to each other in fear of Christ. Does this only apply to our relationships within the body of Christ? I say a loud No, but it could be a so-called haven to practice relationships. If anything, we need to extend our ambassadorship to the world because we are showing ourselves as representatives of Christ.

While participating in a foreign exchange program, I had the opportunity to spend time with an ambassador and his wife in Azerbaijan, the country I was visiting. He and his wife represented the United States. I never understood the role of ambassadorship until I had the opportunity to shadow the ambassador and his wife in their daily life. I spent hours visiting schools with them, listening to the countrymen, hearing their stories, representing my country, sharing my life to serve, and expressing unity, and being an ambassador of Christ. Ambassadorship is a life of Godly representation, joy, sharing, and imparting the living Word to others. It is not a difficult life but a true life, authentic, honest, and heartful. I am representing The Father on this Earth. I am sharing and administering coming alongside the person or persons as God. Ambassadorship is not a work of negotiation, judgment, condemnation, or personal jabs, but acceptance, genuine love, and correct representation. Often, I would walk away from the day enlightened and enamored of the people the ambassador was serving. It was such a powerful experience. I did not speak the people's language, but everyone I encountered understood the care and concern.

All kinds of people loved and hated Jesus. The haters still made Jesus famous, and His presence was known to them. I always want to be like Jesus to the people I encounter because their salvation and mine are at stake. God loves His humanity too much to write them off without giving everyone an opportunity for redemption. We may grow weary, get disgusted, or, worse yet, make a judgment to who should hear about God, but Jesus never did. Our relationship with others starts where our relationship with God leaves off.

> *Luke 10:27 (NLT) tells me, "'Love the Lord your God with all your heart, soul, strength and with all your mind;' and 'Love your neighbor as yourself."*

> *Ephesians 5:21 (NKJV), "Be filled with the spirit, speak in psalms and spiritual songs, and make melody in your heart to the Lord."*

| Prayer |

Father, You call us to relationship with others. Oh, that You will bless and direct my relationships with others every day. May I speak in words that encourage and uplift You daily, so I can enjoy the beauty of being in relationship with others. Draw me to those relationships that are for me and move me away from relationships that are not in line with You. I pray over my times in these special relationships, so I may be the ambassador rightly representing You. I put all my relationships in Your hands so I can hear and move in your direction and not my own. Here you can pray specifically for a relationship you are in, and the direction God is moving in that relationship.
Amen.

How am I in right relationship with others? I am first in relationship with The Father, and I seek those relationships that please Him.

The Power of Forgiveness

"And forgive us our debts. As we forgive our debtors," (Matthew 6:10-14, NKJV). The Lord's Prayer opens with us acknowledging The Father, reverencing God as holy, thanking Him for our daily bread, our food, and then we are instructed to forgive ourselves and others each day. It is interesting before we even really can get into The Lord's Prayer, we must forgive not just others (which is what we would naturally expect) but even ourselves. What does the unforgiveness of ourselves look like?

Not letting go of your past is the result of unforgiveness and even bitterness. You trying to move forward while looking in your rearview mirror will certainly cause you to crash. Preoccupied about what you did wrong, how you could have done better; or opening the painful wounds of your life over and over keeps you bound to your past. The enemy seeks to keep a person tethered to their painful past. You cannot enjoy your future if you are bound by your past. As a result, the evil ungodly spirits of your past become walkways, avenues to attract other controlling and manipulative spirits into our lives. Our past experiences can cause us to relive those experiences repeatedly. Even though you may not ever be able to get rid of the bad memories, you can sever the bad memories of hurt and pain from your life. *"Forgetting those things which are behind..." (Philippians 3:13, NKJV).* We start with forgiving ourselves.

Bitterness in our lives can make us physically sick. Unforgiveness in our lives can come from being disappointed, rejected, victimized, cheated, and lied about to name a few culprits. The writer of *Hebrews 12:14-15, (NKJV)* tells us to *"Pursue peace with all people, and holiness, without which no one will see the Lord: looking carefully lest anyone fall short of the grace of God; lest any root of bitterness springing up cause trouble, and by this many become defiled..."* Do not let bitterness destroy you. I have been disappointed and even rejected by those that should have loved and cared for me. I could nurture that pain by feeding it or cutting it off and ending it. Do not allow your pain to find cover in a bed of bitterness. Forgive yourself and forgive those who have hurt you. Forgiveness is your life source.

Forgiving others is both an expected and required act according to our Father. Why must we forgive others who have hurt us? When I started teaching, I took a teacher education course over a weekend that transformed my teaching life. At the time of the class, I was teaching in a middle school. The course instructed the teachers to give a student a chance to start anew every day. This simple act of forgiveness is transformative. Do you know how freeing forgiveness is? Each day you have a chance to start new. I have had so many students say that is what they love about me as a teacher. You never treat me different because of what I do or what I did yesterday. I have met students sometimes ten years later in the community who remember that kind of grace. One in particular I met at a local restaurant. I did not recognize her, but she remembered not only me but her behavior in my class. Suddenly I had a young woman crying before me. I asked if she was okay. Then she sobbed more as she told me how she spent years wanting to find me to apologize for her middle school behavior. I recognized the name, a little of the face, and then I listened to her. She was ashamed of herself, and she wanted my forgiveness. Again, I was reminded that the gift of forgiveness can transform lives. The power to forgive ourselves and others can save lives and souls. Jesus freed the outcast and brought them into society through the power of forgiveness. Our unforgiveness can hinder our prayers and destroy our communication with God. Keep your heart from offense and learn to forgive.

Matthew 6:10-14 (NKJV) - "Forgive us our debts. As we forgive our debtors."

Hebrews 12:14 (NKJV) – "Pursue peace with all people, and holiness, without which no one will see the Lord."

> **Prayer**
>
> *Lord, teach me to forgive myself and others. Who am I to hold back my forgiveness when You have forgiven me for past, present, and future sins? Thank you for showing Your love for me. I am more than my mistakes in Your eyes. I pray for a new view of myself and others so I can be all that I can be and not be bound to my past. In Jesus' name, Amen*

How do I forgive myself and others? I look to Jesus because He thought I was valuable enough to forgive me even before I was born and die for me. I can only respond to His forgiveness for me and forgive myself and others.

Give Me My Father's Eyes

See me in my potential, not my past. God always sees our potential; we get stuck in our past. Saul was the chosen king of Israel by the Lord. Samuel, the seer, was sent to give Saul his special message from God. *"And I am here to tell you that you and your family are the focus of all of Israel's hopes,"* (First Samuel 9: 20, NLT). Saul replied to Samuel that he was only from the tribe of Benjamin, the smallest tribe of Israel and the least important of all the families of that tribe *(First Samuel 9: 21-22, NLT)*. He even questioned Samuel *"Why are you talking like this to me?"* (First Samuel 9:21). He was appointed the ruler over Israel even though he was not the king of choice by the people. Saul at thirty years of age becomes king and reigns for forty-two years. Sometimes we can miss the beauty of a person (even ourselves) because we cannot see beyond the physical form. God is not bound by our present or past state. The God of the Universe, the Creator knows all of us and invites us to join Him, *"Give me your heart ...And let your eyes delight in my ways,"* (Proverbs 23:26, NIV).

Years ago, as I transitioned to a new school and from teaching high school students to middle school. I experienced something I never experienced. Suddenly I was in an environment that I felt ill equipped to handle. I had tried all my teacher tricks, calling parents, assigning detention, talking to the student, instilling bonus points, but honestly nothing was really working. I spent my evenings on the phone (two hours minimum sometimes) calling the parents of the students who gave me problems. I even resorted to early morning phone calls, but honestly, I felt beat up and defeated. I wondered where these kids came from. I remember crying out to God for revelation like I never had before. My prayer became urgent and desperate. As I would get closer to work each morning, I became absolutely disturbed. A spirit of dread and defeat seemed to be hanging onto me. I remember saying aloud in my car, "I need help Lord. I cannot get past what is happening here with my students." During this prayer I asked for God to give me His eyes. How did He see my students? Who are they to Him compared to what I see? I was sincere and earnest in this request because I knew that unless I could see them like He did I could never get to where I needed to be for them. I said that prayer and kept that prayer always ahead of me.

It wasn't overnight but I came to see that every person, child, is beautiful in God's eyes because God sees who you really are despite yourself. Some of my kids that seemed the worst felt poorly about themselves, so I made an effort to know my students and find that one thing even if it was a small detail about them and learn to see them as Christ. I would stand at my classroom door and guess what every day they got a word from me, a good word. I practiced every day until it changed how I would see them. Some students got special errands because they were fast; others became my in-house artists because they could draw so well. Every student became special in my eyes like God sees each and every one of us. Years later, eighteen years later, I met one of my middle school students and he shared that I believed in him even when his parents never did and that changed his life. Since that time, I have always kept this practice. I will remember details about each student and make that connection because to really teach a student you have to know your students beyond the numbers and the charts to impact their educational potential.

God loves us all. He loves us without the conditions of good or bad, agreeable, or disagreeable, rich, or poor, cute, or ugly and that is amazing. God's love is never conditional, short sighted, or limited. Love is the only debt I should owe my fellow man and only The Father can teach us that kind of love. How we love a person has a lasting impact that effects the person we are tomorrow.

> *First Samuel 26:24 (NKJV) "And indeed, as your life was valued much this day in my eyes, so let my life be valued much in the eyes of the Lord and let Him deliver me out of all tribulation."*

> *Genesis 6:8 (NKJV) "But Noah found grace in the eyes of the Lord."*

> *First Samuel 15:17 (NKJV) "So Samuel said, "When you were little in your own eyes, were you not head of the tribes of Israel? And did not the Lord anoint you king over Israel?"*

Second Kings 6:20 (NKJV) "So it was, when they had come to Samaria, that Elisha said, "Lord, open the eyes of these men, that they may see." And the Lord opened their eyes, and they saw; and there they were, inside Samaria!"

Prayer

Father, I know You love me. You gave Your life for me even before I was even born because of the love You have for me. I need to know how to extend Your love to myself and others. Teach me to love like You Father, so I can extend the love to others. Lord, open my eyes in new ways to see beyond the limits that I have placed on people. Father, give me Your eyes and let me see the beauty of each person that I am in contact starting with myself. Change my perspective.
Amen

How can I love? Love starts with learning the love of The Father for me.

The love of God is endless. So, we must always grow in our love for The Father. In the New Living Translation of *Philippians 1:9*, Paul prays, *"I pray that your love will overflow more and more, and that you will keep on growing in knowledge and understanding."* Growing in our love for The Father starts with knowledge, knowing and understanding The Father. For us as humans we know the value of a person increases with us spending time with the person, talking, and communing with our loved one to know and understand them. The more time we spend with the person we love our love grows more strongly. The same is true with our love for The Father overtime our love for The Father grows with talking and communing to know and understand Him. Secondly, our love must have an object of love. Jesus loved His disciples, and He loves us. *First John 4:7 (NLT)* tells us, *"Dear friends, let us continue to love one another, for love comes from God. Anyone who loves is a child of God and knows God."* It is how we love that distinguishes us as a child of God. As the Beatles song says, "all you need is love." Reach out and love others. In *John 15:13 (NLT)* we are reminded, *"This is my commandment: Love each other in the same way I have loved you. There is no greater love than to lay down one's life for one's friends."* Love requires sacrifice. Jesus sacrificed His life because He loves us. Loving The Father as we are to love others is sacrificial. Sacrificial means I willingly put the person before me.

As we close our spiritual journey for now, we know that in everything we encounter, God is with us every time. There are no surprises in God's economy or in anything we can encounter. Grab hold of God's Words and know that He never fails. I leave you with this final prayer my daughter penned for me as I went back to school during the pandemic of 2020-2021. The words resound for me; and I trust they will for you. You are part of a greater community. We surround and support the journey God has given you and all of us to fulfill the greatest purpose on this Earth.

Ashley's Prayer - **A Message for You**

You are facing many obstacles and many battles. Situations and people that try to tear you down, but with planning and strength you will have the power to overcome. Things appear bleak but there is hope and you are divinely guided and helped. Call for help and support, you are part of a greater team of souls and angels who are ready to come alongside of you. I love you, Mom. Stay safe and well

About the Author

Dr. Yvette Avery has been a follower of Christ for over 40 years. She is a national board-certified English educator and has been a published technical writer of curriculum and college assessments, and mentor educator for over 30 years. She is a mother of three adult daughters and has a feisty Bichon dog, Titus. She presently works as a high school English teacher in the public school system in Florida.

Dr. Avery has served her church and community through mentoring and discipleship of young women and incarcerated individuals. She has served as a Bible study leader and prayer counselor in several churches, and as an overseas missionary. Her passion is to share the love of Christ by affirming and empowering people groups to embrace their unique gifts and talents to fulfill their purpose.

Dr. Avery earned her Doctor of Philosophy degree in curriculum and instruction, evaluation, and research, and an Educational Specialist degree in gifted education and curriculum instruction from Barry University, in Miami, Florida. Her Master's degree is in English education and TESOL (Teaching English to Speakers of Other Languages) from Nova Southeastern University, Davie, Florida. She has served on several national committees to review and develop national curricula for secondary school students throughout the U.S.

She is an avid traveler and art lover and can be found visiting a museum or a local art show opening. She resides in Fort Lauderdale, Florida where she pursues her writing when not teaching.